T0275035

Advance Praise for *The View from My Foxhole*

"Twenty-seven months and three bloody Pacific Operation campaigns changed a young man excited about the adventure of foreign places to an experienced combat Marine survivor relieved to claim a seat on a magic ship stateside. William Swanson's firsthand account of life in jungle foxholes and ship bellies tells of the real life of those lucky enough to make it through another day of WWII in the Pacific: lack of food, water, safety, any kind of comfort. A combat Marine doesn't ask why, just does his job well. A good read written with a rare blend of practicality, authenticity, and humanity."

—**Cynthia Kraack, award-winning author
and co-writer,** *40 Thieves on Saipan*

THE
VIEW FROM
MY FOXHOLE

THE

VIEW FROM MY FOXHOLE

A MARINE PRIVATE'S FIRSTHAND WORLD WAR II COMBAT EXPERIENCE FROM GUADALCANAL TO IWO JIMA

WILLIAM SWANSON

PERMUTED
PRESS

A PERMUTED PRESS BOOK
ISBN: 978-1-63758-467-5
ISBN (eBook): 978-1-63758-468-2

The View from My Foxhole:
A Marine Private's Firsthand World War II Combat
Experience from Guadalcanal to Iwo Jima
© 2022 by William Swanson
All Rights Reserved

Interior Design by Yoni Limor

All people, locations, events, and situations are portrayed to the best of the author's memory. While all of the events described are true, some names and identifying details have been changed to protect the privacy of the people involved.

No part of this book may be reproduced, stored in a retrieval system, or transmitted by any means without the written permission of the author and publisher.

PERMUTED
PRESS

Permuted Press, LLC
New York • Nashville
permutedpress.com

Published in the United States of America
1 2 3 4 5 6 7 8 9 10

Dedicated, first and foremost,
to those whose luck ran out and, second,
to a couple of old companions: misery and fear.

NOTE FROM THE PUBLISHER

This book is a memoir. It reflects the author's recollections of experiences that occurred decades prior. Some language may be offensive to some readers, including the term "Jap," which the author uses to refer to the enemy and not as a racial or ethnic slur. In fact, prior to World War II, the term was not considered offensive—it was only after the war that it was considered a derogatory insult. The author displays respect for the enemy's determination and bravery.

TABLE CONTENTS

PREFACE

This is the true story of a not-so-casual journey across the Pacific while on a tour of duty in the United States Marine Corps, 1942–1945. Although conceding that this not to be confused with real literature, I hope that in some way I have been able to convey a feeling of what it was to be an ordinary rifleman in that rather hard and sometimes dangerous time. This is not about heroes or of heroic deeds. It is, instead, about an occasional bit of misery and those bone-weary foot sloggers who—upon finding themselves in terrible circumstances and even when wishing to hell they were somewhere else—did what they had to do.

Though some stories were sadder and more difficult than mine, some funnier than mine, and many more pleasant than mine, this, to the best of my recollection, is how the thing looked from my particular foxhole.

"Under certain circumstances, urgent circumstances, desperate circumstances, profanity provides a relief denied even to prayer."

Mark Twain 1835–1910

SAILINGS

November 1942, embarked USS *Arthur Middleton* for practice landings on the Southern California coast.

January 1943, embarked USS *Mount Vernon* bound for New Zealand.

March 1943, embarked USS *President Hayes* for practice landings on the New Zealand coast.

June 1943, embarked USS *George Clymer* bound for Guadalcanal, BSI.

October 1943, embarked USS *Crescent City* bound for the invasion of Bougainville, BSI.

January 1944, embarked USS *President Hayes* for a return to Guadalcanal, BSI.

March 1944, embarked USS *President Adams* bound for an aborted invasion of New Ireland.

June 1944, embarked USS *President Hayes* bound for the invasion of Guam.

February 1945, embarked USS *Fayette* bound for the invasion of Iwo Jima.

February 1945, evacuated to the USS *Doyen*, then transferred to the USS *President Adams* bound for Saipan.

March 1945, embarked USS *Karnes* bound for Pearl Harbor.

April 1945, embarked USS *Matsonia* bound for San Francisco.

Misery, the damned thing seemed to hit with an utter, almost callous disregard. But fear—I learned soon enough to envy those who had no fear.

SAN DIEGO

*In the beginning, there will be the illusion
of excitement and adventure.*

Turning eighteen in 1942 was, for some, just about
the right age at just about the right time—prime
time, many would say. The depression was over
and the war was on as I graduated from high school in
June, read about the Marines landing on Guadalcanal
on August 7, and then reached my eighteenth birthday
on August 10. It has been said that this was the best
of times and the worst of times, and that sums it up
pretty well. For a rather large number of us prime-tim-
ers, this best of times had to do with great excitement,
with thoughts of high adventure. And we could hardly wait to get in the damn thing. The worst of times
would come later, but we scarcely gave it a thought.
Why I chose the Marine Corps, I can't really say, except that it probably had to do with their unique "esprit de corps" along with a reputation of being first
to fight. Then, compounding the thing, I ran into a

couple of former "China Marines" along the way, giving me my first inkling of this "once a Marine, always a Marine" business and, at the same time, only reinforcing that expectation of high adventure. So, it is no doubt a combination of these events and fate that brings me to this particular date and place.

A side note to all this is that I wouldn't take a million for the memories, the experiences, and the camaraderie but wouldn't do it again for all the Goddamn tea in China.

September 17, 1942

I arrive in Los Angeles for a final physical and signing of papers before being sworn into service in the US Marine Corps. It is a long, drawn-out session and no doubt pretty routine, but we detect a not-so-subtle change after the official swearing in. Up to this point, we have been asked to do this or that. Now, however, we are told, in no uncertain terms, what to do and when to do it. A sort of major line has been crossed and nothing will ever be the same.

The paperwork is finally finished around nine or so, and we are then hustled aboard a Greyhound bus for the trip to our new home, the Marine Corps Recruit Depot in San Diego. Arriving after midnight, the bus stops at a deserted part of the base, which seems odd. I guess we had expected to drive in the main gate, but this isolated location merely sets the stage for our "welcome." The driver quickly opens the door, and a loud gruff voice immediately yells "fall out." Unfortunately (for us), we fail to grasp the rather simple import of this new term and, instead, fumble around getting our gear together, totally unaware of the wretched turn our lives are about to take.

The voice, sounding very impatient now, speaks again, and this time there is no mistaking the message. "Get your Goddamn candy asses off this bus and be damned quick about it. You're in the United States Marine Corps now, and when you're given an order, you had better jump and damned fast." That gets our attention, and we stumble out of the bus as fast as we can, being cursed and berated every step of the way. Can't figure what could have brought on such an awful tirade. We are still blissfully unaware that this is the way it will be for most of the next two months and is just one part of a process which is designed to turn ordinary people into Marines. At this moment, however, we are beginning to wonder if we might not have made a rather serious and—perhaps worst of all—irrevocable mistake.

"All right, you dirty, no-good sons of bitches, form into three rows and shut your Goddamned mouths." The voice belongs to a man in a khaki uniform, wearing a campaign hat and carrying a swagger stick—a sergeant, we guess. He just stands there looking at us for several minutes, like he is some sort of god or perhaps higher, and he looks disgusted at what he sees. "Of all the rotten, stinking, low-life bastards I've ever seen, you are undoubtedly the worst. What in the Goddamn hell makes you people think you could ever be a pimple on a real Marine's ass? Look at you! Son of a bitch, I can't believe the likes of you actually had the nerve to join the Marine Corps. God help us all if it is up to you miserable bastards to defend this country."

This rather unfriendly greeting goes on and on until we finally hit bottom and begin to feel that maybe we are the worst he's ever seen. We are all volunteers, although a few joined up to escape being drafted into the Army and they are, perhaps, sickest of all—feeling that, in hindsight, they should have chosen the frying pan. Even so, after having literally signed our lives away in order to fight for our country, we sort of thought the Marine Corps might look kindly on our sacrifice and even be a little bit glad to see us. Never in our wildest dreams could we have imagined a reception like this.

The sergeant, or the almighty, whatever the hell he calls himself, finally gets tired of giving us hell and we are then marched over to a large building. Inside, another surly Marine orders us to turn in all our possessions. He says we are to keep nothing. Going to prison could hardly be worse, and we note that, since our arrival in San Diego, we have yet to hear anything even resembling a kind word. Next, we are led to a large room with many bunks and told to find a sack, this being Marine Corps lingo for a bed, and it comes as no surprise that these sacks have to be made up from scratch. The next bit of good news is that reveille will be at 0500 hours, that we are to be dressed and shaved by 0515, and we are, by now, quite sure they mean what they say. Looking back on this, our first day in the Marine Corps, disaster seems to be the word that pops up most often, although there is some disagreement about the term even coming close to describing the day. We turn in wondering what in the Goddamned hell we have let ourselves in for. It is a short night.

After a few minutes, or so it seems, we are rudely wakened by a horrible, incredible sound. Our wakeup call is a recording of the entire Marine band playing reveille, and the noise literally blows us out of our sacks. This is the beginning of our stay in boot camp, and as the days go by, we learn what being a Marine is all about. Unfortunately, life doesn't get any better for a while. Sad to say, it actually gets worse. But very slowly, and sometimes reluctantly, we learn that it is easier and a bit more pleasant when we do it their way.

During these first days, we are issued dungarees and dress greens for inspections (they apparently do not know what the word "liberty" means) along with a variety of other gear including a new Garand rifle. Naturally, this rifle is covered with a heavy coat of cosmoline and is a real bearcat to clean. They apparently do not realize just how miserably hard it is to get the damn stuff off and, seemingly quite the opposite in fact, expect and even insist that the rifle be spotless in short order. There is a momentary thought of trying to convey this information to them, but after considering their response to previous efforts at enlightenment, this is not pursued. Instead, we tackle the job with an unaccustomed gusto and, as time goes by, learn that given the proper incentive, it is possible to do a great variety of miserable and distasteful chores. At this time and on many future occasions, it is stressed that, if you take care of your rifle, your rifle will take care of you, and they show extreme displeasure when you fail to do this properly.

In addition to this rifle #338252 (a number, along with my serial number, that will be etched in my mem-

16

ory forever) and bayonet, we are issued "782 gear" and given a bucket of stuff. The term "782 gear" is more Gyrene lingo and has to do with packs, cartridge belts, canteens, entrenching tools, and the like. The stuff they give us is mostly personal items which the Marine Corps thinks we should have. There is, of course, a reason behind these "gifts" and it pretty much has to do with the fact that this place has very few of the amenities normally associated with civilization. Then, adding some small insult to injury, our first payday confirms an ugly rumor that the items in the bucket were not really gifts at all.

We are also issued a pair of dog tags to be worn at all times. These being small, oval-shaped brass discs which have our name, serial number, religion, date of last tetanus shot, blood type, and whether regular or reserve stamped on. They are to be worn around our necks with one in a separate loop so that, in case of an untimely death, that one can be cut or yanked off for records purposes while the other stays with the body. They do think of everything.

Next, we are placed in groups of sixty, called platoons (not the same as platoons in a rifle company, which have about forty men). Each of these platoons stays together for the duration of boot camp and is led by a sergeant, called a DI (for drill instructor). He is not an officer but expects to be treated like one, only more so, and there is much unpleasantness for those who fail to recognize that simple fact. The idea is to begin thinking and acting as a team rather than as individuals, and slowly but surely, we get the knack of keeping in step. The days are long, the training rough and sometimes brutal, and it is becoming increasingly clear that the lot of the rifleman is a hard one.

Long lines and waiting are the order of the day—waiting for chow, waiting to shave, shower, to hit the head (visit the latrine). Waiting for a plethora of shots and dreading the oft-discussed square needle (it was only a rumor, thank God). Waiting for the sergeant to give us hell and not being disappointed.

"Yer left, yer left—you had a good home but you left. I said yer left, Goddammit, yer left. Haven't you bastards learned a Goddamn thing?" The sergeant curses and rails at our inability to keep in step.

Each day, however, we seem to fumble and stumble a little less, though our DI continually complains that we are lagging behind the other platoons and causing him no end of embarrassment. He says that he has never had a platoon fail to get through boot camp, but that we are so Godawful lousy we just might spoil his record. He indicates that the easy days are therefore over, that we are going to have to work longer and harder, including our time off. "Jesus Christ," what in the hell easy days is he talking about—and we don't have any Goddamned time off!

In truth, we are probably about average, and all the platoons are no doubt given the benefit of a similar incentive. Nevertheless, he keeps his promise. We do work harder and longer and, in addition, are often roused out at night, our only time off, for such things as calisthenics or, when he is in an especially foul mood, seabag inspection. This means we are required to lay our complete issue of gear and clothing out in the company street, all folded and stacked neatly as well as being in an exact and particular order. Up and on shoulders, a rather tiring drill with the rifle and a special favorite of our DI, and it continues to be a quite regular nighttime activity.

These interruptions are, of course, not happy times and occur most often after midnight, which just happens to coincide with the closing of the non-commissioned officers' club. Though we speculate on this apparent coincidence among ourselves, it is never mentioned in the sergeant's presence—we have learned something.

Then a day when it all comes together, a day when the whole Goddamned platoon is in step. To the rear, column right, to the winds, left shoulder arms—we are doing it all. There is a new lilt in our step, an ease in our movements as we execute each command. The merest hint of a smile crosses the sergeant's face.

Eventually, but not easily, we get through the first month of this rather nasty metamorphosis and are then transferred to the rifle range at Camp Matthews, where our lives actually begin to get a little better. We are not yet considered Marines but seemingly have had a small promotion to human being, and we are thankful for any small favors. I particularly enjoy our time on the range and am fortunate enough to shoot "expert" which, in addition to a little prestige, adds five dollars to my fifty-a-month private's pay.

We spend three weeks at Camp Matthews and, in so doing, recoup a bit of our tattered self-image, although the hammer comes down just often enough that we avoid letting this newfound status of human being delude us into thinking we are anything but "boots." In the view of actual Marines, we are still bottom of the bottom, although it is a comfort to know that there are now those who are even lower than us.

Finally, with rifle training out of the way, we move back to the recruit depot for our last two weeks of boot camp and then "graduation." And now, here's one for the books: after all the miserable Goddamned hell our DI put us through, we actually took up a collection and gave the son of a bitch a watch.

This, however, is only the first of many emotions that I will wonder about as I serve out my hitch in the Corps. And, speaking of hitches, did I mention the big fat hog I cut in the ass (an expression picked up from my Tennessee buddies) by signing up for four years instead of the war and out as most did? Best that I not even attempt to explain that one. However, it all somehow fits together, and I doubt there is a better example of a love-hate relationship than exists in the Marine Corps.

This so-called graduation completes the first part of a rather amazing transformation. I don't quite know how it is done, but people come into this place and come out transformed. There is a sense of pride instilled over and above the suffering, and even though we have learned to hate the Goddamn outfit with a passion, this is somehow pushed aside by the feeling that we are finally one of them. "Once a Marine, always a Marine" has its beginning in pain and misery.

On the way to our first liberty, we pass a group of new "boots" and cannot believe that we actually looked like them only two months ago. What a ragtag bunch, they'd never make it in the "Old Corps." We welcome them with the same words we were welcomed with: "You'll be sorrrry!" It is a relief getting through boot camp and, although much worse is to come, we are now Marines—at least in our view.

With that first liberty over all too soon, including a great trip home for me, most of us report to the new Marine Corps base at Camp Pendleton. Some, like myself, are then assigned to the Ninth Marine Regiment, the Ninth being one of three line regiments making up the Third Marine Division. I am further ordered to one of the rifle companies and placed in the second platoon, which will be my home for the next two and half years. Being a new "boot," I draw the job of assistant BAR man, which means I carry my own M1 rifle, cartridge belt, and assorted gear, and, in addition, get to wear a bandoleer containing twelve twenty-round magazines for the BAR (Browning Automatic Rifle). This not being a particularly sought-after position, I manage to hold on to it for the next year or so, although I will have more than a passing acquaintance with most every job in the platoon before it's over.

November and December are busy months with numerous field problems and much time spent on obstacle courses and endurance runs. However, part of our training necessarily has to do with getting from ship to shore, and I arrive at Pendleton just in time to join the regiment for a two-week stint aboard ship. Our particular troop transport is the USS *Arthur Middleton* and is only the first of many that I will get to know. After boarding, we immediately head below to our troop compartment and encounter, for the first time, that unique combination of stale salt air, fuel oil, cooking, and assorted other odors which give shipboard life its rather distinctive aroma. The aroma is even more distinctive on the lower decks.

There is much to learn in this phase of our training, and we soon find that climbing down landing nets with pack and weapons is not only difficult but often dangerous. Another little fact, which we are quickly made aware of, is that the only way back on board is by climbing up the damned nets, and that is plain hard work. However, we eventually get the hang of this up-and-down-nets business and, although our many practice landings go reasonably well, I, along with a few others, get well acquainted with the miserable miseries of mal de mer—or sea sickness.

These good times do not last, however, and our luck finally runs out as plans are being made for a last trip down the nets. The weather has taken a sudden turn for the worse, and this particular landing is to be made under cover of darkness. The best, it seems, is always saved for last. A night landing in decent weather probably wouldn't be too bad, and a stormy landing in daylight might even be tolerable, but going down the nets at night in this storm seems like madness, at least to us. And with old salts getting sick in the pitching and rolling of the ship, the term miserable seems totally inadequate in describing the condition of us landlubbers. We continue to hope the operation will be canceled or at least postponed until daylight. The Marine Corps, however, has other ideas and seems determined that we should learn a little of the fine art of suffering.

Finally, then, our silent pleas having fallen on deaf ears, the ship's crew gets the word and around midnight begins moving the twenty-odd landing craft (Higgins boats) from positions on deck and in davits into the rather unfriendly ocean. And it is not an easy time. As the winches raise them off the deck, the wind sends the boats crashing into the superstructure or whatever is nearby. In this resultant turmoil, the ship suffers a fair amount of damage but, difficulties notwithstanding, the boats are finally lowered to the water, and we are ordered to report to our assigned debarking station (landing net).

Leaving the interior of the ship, we pass through the double set of blackout curtains and are soaked in seconds. That, along with our first look at the black night and the feel of wind and rain, quickly confirms earlier suspicions that this little exercise is going to be a real son of a bitch. And occasional glimpses of the ocean do nothing to dispel this notion; the Goddamn swells look huge.

Railside, looking down at the dark water, we cannot believe they really mean to send us down in this weather. Maybe they just want to scare us a little. Now the coxswain, having finally maneuvered his boat below our net (no small feat this night), must try to maintain his position against the surging sea. Over the sound of the storm, we can hear that distinctive roar as he guns the engine, moving forward and back trying to keep on station. Then, as our eyes get more accustomed to the dark, we begin to get some idea of just what it is that we are being asked—the right word is "ordered"—to do.

Our Higgins boat appears to drop twenty feet or so into a sort of trough then, as the swells catch it, rises up with the sea and crashes into the side of the ship—this with a horrible, grinding noise. This upward movement carries the boat almost to the rail, then it literally drops out of sight as the sea subsides. It doesn't seem possible that we can get down the ragged-looking net without being crunched between boat and ship, thrown into the stormy ocean, or, at the very least, just falling down in the damned boat. If they mean to scare us, they are doing a good job of it. In addition, many of us have, by now, passed beyond seasickness into feeling miserable as hell.

"Now hear this," the command is almost lost in the wind and rain. "Commence debarkation." Dirty son of a bitch, they're really going to do it! We stop worrying about whether and start worrying about how. Two of the older hands are ordered to go first and we watch, hoping to learn from them, but they are soon out of sight and we know little more than before. Once in the boat, their job is to hold the net as taut as possible, pulling down as the boat rises, then letting out slack as it falls.

My turn, and it's kind of scary as I put a leg over the rail and try to find a decent foothold. All I can think of is that damned boat smashing into the ship and trying not to be caught in between. The important thing, we are told, is to step off as the boat is rising and not as it is falling. Sounds easy enough but, with the boat moving so fast, you have to be damn quick. I try to step off near the top of one rise but am too late and the boat drops away, leaving me hanging by my hands. Scrambling to secure my feet, I vow to catch the next up movement for sure, and I get lucky on that effort, sort of half-falling into the boat.

Our platoon finally gets down without serious mishap, the net is thrown over the side, and the coxswain heads into the dark. However, we soon lose sight of the ship and, for the first time, realize just how small and insignificant we are as our little boat tries to hold its own in the heavy seas. Down in the troughs, the swells seem to tower over us, and we begin to have serious doubts about this thing actually making it to the beach. If we were soaked before, we are now drenched as the rain continues and seawater sprays over the gunwales and front ramp. One feature of these boats that was discovered early on and that we are emphatically re-discovering this night is that, in design, comfort took a decided back seat (if considered at all), as there is no place to sit or room to do so, even if we tried. There is room only to stand, and this shoulder to shoulder. The damn things, instead of riding over the seas, seem to prefer the troughs and just sort of smash into the waves, or is it vice versa? Either way, we take a beating.

However, and in spite of it all, we somehow manage to rendezvous with the other boats in our group and begin circling. Waiting for further instructions, I am so damn sick by this time that I don't care which end is up, and I have plenty of company. The only thing on my mind is getting out of this damned boat and onto something that doesn't move in six directions at once. Finally, after what seemed like an eternity of pounding and bouncing, the boats somehow get the word, peel out of their circular pattern into a sort of ragged line, and head for the beach. It is a rough surf, and our boat almost broaches (turns sideways) as we approach the shore. But the ramp finally clanks down, and we struggle through the waves onto somewhat dry land. We still have a long, rough day ahead, as dawn is just breaking. But thank God, the night and that damn boat ride are over. Already, it looks like I have chosen a hard and dangerous business and, the real hell of it is, I don't even know the meaning of the words—yet.

Returning to Pendleton, we get back into constant, rigorous training, and although the days are hard, evening usually finds us heading for the slop-chute and a little relaxation. Slop-chute being Marine Corps lingo for the enlisted men's pub, which serves beer and snacks. It isn't much of a place, the camp being still under construction, but it gives us a chance to unwind and complain about the damned officers and our so-called miserable lives. Miserable—now there is another interesting word and one whose meaning we are destined to explore in depth.

The first part of December sees our regiment on the move again, this time to the scout and sniper school at San Onofre. This is a two-week course that gets down to the real nitty-gritty of infantry fighting and is about as rough as they could make it. However, we learn and are toughened in the process. Some of our newfound skills include rappelling down sheer cliffs, getting over and under barbed-wire entanglements, knife fighting, advanced judo, and a good deal of time spent with the bayonet. They have come up with a dandy method for getting over barbed wire, and that is for one of us to fall on the damn stuff while the others leap over, using that "lucky" individual as a stepping stone. Surprisingly, it works pretty well but is a bit disconcerting on the first try. The training gets downright mean and dirty in an attempt to be realistic, but we are slowly learning that "mean" is what this business is all about.

The last day finds us crawling on our bellies over a half mile or so of rock and brush with live machine-gun fire—a gentle reminder to keep our heads down. All in all, it has been an advanced course on how best to do your enemy in. The main thrust of the thing is to do it before the son of a bitch does it to you.

Back at the main camp, it's Christmas and we have been granted, reluctantly no doubt, a two-day liberty. Those of us from around here are particularly lucky as we have a chance to get home for this special day. The holiday get-together with family is wonderful, and I hate to see it end, but my big adventure is waiting and is to begin sooner than expected. In truth, it will be two and a half years and a lot of water under the bridge before I see home again.

Getting back to camp, however, is the immediate problem. With gasoline rationing now a fact of life, along with the military using much of the transportation system, getting back to bases and ships is a real challenge, especially during the holidays. Using some of their precious gasoline, my folks drive me to downtown Glendale, where we say our goodbyes and I take the red streetcar into LA. As expected, the bus and train stations are packed to overflowing, so I wind up taking a streetcar to Santa Ana and hitchhiking the rest of the way. Nothing, it seems, is easy these days.

Returning once again to Pendleton, rumors abound, and I feel a new excitement in the air. Although training goes on all day and sometimes all night as we prepare for the tough times ahead, working parties are now regularly detailed to San Diego Harbor, and we begin to wonder if it is our gear that is being moved about. Then, toward the end of that first week in January, the suspense is finally lifted as we are suddenly restricted to camp and informed that the regiment is shipping out. There will be no more liberty, no phone calls, and our mail is to be censored from now on. The saying goes that "a slip of the lip might sink a ship" and, in this case, the ship could be ours.

NEW ZEALAND

Home will be that place where the infan-
tryman puts his helmet.

January 23, 1943

Leaving Camp Pendleton by train, we arrive at the
Broadway Street Pier in San Diego and immediately board the USS *Mount Vernon*. It has been raining
all day and continues as we embark. An ominous sign,
perhaps, but we are glad to be moving out, though we
briefly wonder which of us will return.

"Now hear this on the duty watch, set conditions
for sea."

There is no band, no cheering crowd, or fanfare of
any kind. Only a gloomy, steady rain as the ship pulls
away from the dock and we take a last look at home.
The adventure begins, but what will it be? Our ship
clears the harbor as dusk settles and is sailing without

escort, relying only on her speed to elude enemy subs. However, there are no untoward incidents, and the two-week voyage is a pleasant one.

The first morning brings news that our destination is Auckland, New Zealand. Most are happy with that, although some, thinking they were going to get a crack at the Japs right away, are disappointed.

As might be expected, many of us are seasick during the first few days, but sacking out is not allowed. Instead, we are kept busy with calisthenics, school on weapons, tactics, and other duties and, with that rather forced activity, soon get our sea legs. Now, with the misery over, we find that life at sea is not too bad, and we even learn to enjoy the gentle roll of the ship. Being the SS *Washington* in peacetime, she is one of the larger troop transports and carries our reinforced regiment of some five thousand men. This means long chow lines and, as a matter of fact, long lines for everything, and there is at least a two-hour wait for each meal. By necessity, dining is pretty basic and there are no white tablecloths, at least not for us. There are no chairs either as mealtime on troop transports is strictly a stand-up affair. For the most part, however, the voyage is a welcome relief from hard training, and we make the most of our small vacation.

Afternoon usually finds the regimental band practicing on the promenade deck, mixing songs like "Amapola," "Green Eyes," and "Beer Barrel Polka" with the "Washington Post March" and "Semper Fidelis." Although the band will not be part of future voyages, it is a pleasant time, and we often stand by the rail, shooting the breeze or just watching the ocean roll by.

In keeping with the general spirit of things, flying fish even get in the act as groups of twenty or thirty take off in unison, fly maybe fifty feet or so, and then drop back in the water. Dolphins also provide company and diversion as they swim alongside, seemingly escorting and urging us on. It is all very peaceful, like a lull before a storm—a storm that is sure to come.

We cross the equator as well as the International Date Line on this cruise, and in so doing, are allowed to enter the Mystical Kingdom of the deep and forever hold the title of "Shellback." However, the old salts feel that the ship is far too limited for an adequate initiation, so our official induction into this ancient order will take place in a muddy, marshy lagoon in New Zealand with an old beer-bellied gunnery sergeant taking the part of King Neptune. Ugh, it is almost too horrible to contemplate.

The ship stops at the mouth of Auckland Harbor and a local pilot is taken aboard to guide us through the protective minefields. Then, as we move into the dock, a New Zealand army band strikes up the Marine Hymn. It is a nice welcome and we enjoy it—the probability being that future welcoming committees will be of a different sort. As soon as the ship is secured, we disembark and travel by train to the small town of Papakura, located some twenty miles south of Auckland. From there, we march a few miles to our new home, a former NZ army base called Camp Hilldene. It's a rather nice camp, being made up of four-man wooden huts and much better than we expected.

Most of our stay is spent in hard, rigorous training with several three-day, sixty-mile hikes in full pack and equipment thrown in for good measure. However, we are seldom away from the sea for long, and the middle of March finds us aboard ship once again. This time, it is the USS *President Hayes* and a week of practice landings along the New Zealand coast. We manage to get down the nets several times during the week, but the weather is reasonably good and the landings mostly routine—just a lot of hard work and discomfort, both of which we are getting to know quite well. After hitting the beach on these little outings, we often dig foxholes and then are required to fill them in. We complain about this extra work, thinking it will be easier when we can just leave the damned things and move on—or will it?

Finishing out our week aboard ship, we return to Camp Hilldene and more training, more inspections, and all the other good stuff. Speaking of inspections, they are a Marine Corps must and are held on Saturday mornings, always. It is normal that a certain amount of discomfort is associated with these events, but here, in particular, they are a damned misery as our only parade ground is a Goddamned cow pasture. The uniform of the day usually calls for dress greens. As you might imagine after marching around in the stuff a couple of hours, the cursing and griping that goes along with the cleanup is just Godawful—which brings me to the subject of attitude. This is an important part of Marine Corps thinking, with the process of promoting and nurturing a proper state of mind beginning early on—stepping off the bus in boot camp being a good example. By now, we are well aware that they are not above being mean and ornery in the pursuit of this objective, and we consider the wearing of dress uniforms in the cow pasture to be a logical, albeit, very minor result of this thinking. In a word, their aim, the very essence of their game, it seems, is to keep us pissed off, with the ultimate goal of directing this anger at the enemy. Meanwhile, though they take a small risk in turning this ire on themselves, they do hold a very large hammer and have not the slightest qualms about using it. Most amazing of all, however, is that the pride of belonging to and being a part of whatever in hell this outfit is somehow overcomes the misery and, when they play that epitome of shipping-over music, the Marine Hymn, we still try to stand a little taller.

A short word is perhaps in order about sixty-mile hikes—the three-day, regimental kind with full pack and weapons. They are, at best, long and tiring, and especially so for those having the misfortune of bringing up the rear. Why in the Goddamn hell is it always us? Anyway, as anyone who has ever been involved in one of these things well knows, the rear of long columns always gets the shaft. Normal procedure calls for a ten-minute break every hour or so on routine marches, and this is usually done. The problem being that these long columns stretch out considerably during a march, which means that by the time the rear ranks close up, the damned break is over and it's movin'-out time again. This, quite naturally, does not set well with those in the rear, resulting in much anger and cursing but it is all for naught—the Goddamned column moves out, and that is that.

So, it is probably not too surprising that toward the end of the last day we are bushed, with many limping

along on sore feet but refusing to fall out. It helps some
that we sing, as men like us have no doubt done for
thousands of years, with these efforts running the gam-
ut from bawdy and even dirty to sentimental and sad.
"That Old Gang of Mine," "My Buddy," and, of course,
"Bless 'Em All" with its many and varied verses are old
standbys. However, the little ditty that comes so naturally when we are really beat down is that old classic of
weary men off on dangerous business. It's called "Show
Me the Way to Go Home," and the title tells you all you
really need to know. Plaintive notes by tired men these
surely are, yet over and above the weariness one cannot
help but notice an unmistakable tinge of pride as these
raggedy-assed bastards plod along.

Landings, long hikes, and parades are only a part
of it, however, and most of our days involve field ex-
ercises of one kind or another. The Marine Corps
calls these things field problems, and they certainly
are that, with some being a bit more so than others.
One of these in particular, a nighttime thing, almost
gets us in the soup. This being an exercise in maintaining contact and direction after dark in a combat
situation, talking and lights are, of course, not allowed.
The problem part begins early on, with my platoon
getting separated from the rest of the company, and
the thing just goes downhill from there. As a matter of
fact, sometime in the wee hours and after much stum-
bling and falling, we find ourselves moving and sliding
down a very steep slope.

We continue like this for some time, hanging on to
each other for support and to maintain contact, all the
while wondering what in the hell we might be walking

or sliding into, until the platoon leader, finally realizing we are hopelessly lost, calls a halt. Though welcome news, we are still in a miserably uncomfortable position due to this steep slope, so we just do what we can in the pitch dark, hoping for an early dawn. Getting behind a tree solves the problem of rolling down the hill, but is of not much help otherwise. To say the least, it is a long miserable night, our brush with the soup coming with daylight as I discover a fifty-foot cliff only a step or two from my tree. We never did completely solve this nighttime wandering-around business, but we continue to find that a little luck is a handy thing.

Though the days are busy and tiring, it really is good duty here, and we are usually allowed a short liberty two or three nights a week. These trips to Papakura are always looked forward to, camp food being nothing to write home about unless you happen to have a fondness for mutton, and we eagerly accept the opportunity to gorge ourselves on steak, eggs, and chips. At the same time, although we are no doubt good for business, the townspeople must do their shopping early as we pretty much clean the place out. We are a hungry bunch, and there are a lot of us. I must say, however, that they treat us very kindly and show a surprising degree of tolerance. We also manage to take the train to Auckland about once a month, usually dining at the King's or the Queen's Cafe, depending on the shape of our wallets so, all in all, it would be hard to find a better place to be stationed. Our only regret is the fact that we came here straight from the States instead of later when we really would have appreciated the place. As things turn out, we are to have no more liberty after our stay in New Zealand and will spend almost two long years in the boondocks.

No story about Marines would be complete without at least a mention of girls and how much we miss them. We long to be with them, even just to be near them, and if we could touch them, wow! Some, as it has always been I guess, do seem to find them but these happy encounters are, for the most part, reserved for a relatively few lucky or perhaps persistent ones. The hard truth being that there are just too damn many of us and too few of them. Making it all the worse, most of us are in our late teens and far from home—the very worst of times to be away from them. We do, however, talk about them, dream about them, and think about them constantly. These easy months here in New Zealand are only the beginning, though, as those who somehow manage to stay in one piece over the next couple of years will discover. We cannot see what lies ahead, but if we could, there would be no girls in the picture after NZ—not even for the lucky/persistent ones. There will be an occasional tantalizing view from afar when one of the more adventurous entertainers drops in, but these rare glimpses will be few and far between and will afford only momentary satisfaction. For our division, at least, it is to be a long, bitter war and will be made the worse by the almost complete absence of these delightful creatures.

Evenings in camp are for writing letters, thinking of home, and wondering where all this is taking us and how it is to end. I wonder how long my luck will last and—the closer we get to it—what the fighting will really be like.

GUADALCANAL

That the infantryman will be denied that oft desired glimpse into the future is fortunate.

June 1943

Ship loading time again as we board the USS *George Clymer* bound for Guadalcanal, British Solomon Islands. At least they were British, now the Japs have most of them, and I imagine part of our job will be to take them back. Our destination being in the heart of the war zone, we sail in convoy and spend much of our free time watching the other transports plow through the seas while destroyers steam back and forth on our flanks. Now and then we see larger warships on the horizon, try to guess where they might be headed, and finally begin to feel as if we really are a part of this gigantic effort. The adventure continues but, like the man said, "you ain't seen nuthin' yet."

A couple of days out, the convoy hits stormy seas and life gets a bit uncomfortable for us troops, with the worst of it being those times that we are ordered to stay below. A lot of the discomfort is due to the simple fact that our bunks are stacked five and six high with only a narrow passageway in between, meaning that the damn troop compartments are crowded and, I might add, hot as the proverbial hubs of Hell. When we are allowed on the weather decks, however, it's kind of fun watching the bow plunge into the heavy seas and then hearing the odd whine of the screws as they are momentarily forced out of the water. Although the look of ocean in storm is always ominous, this rather uneasy feeling seems even more pronounced in these dangerous times. Evening, in particular, with darkening sky and murky water, brings a deep sense of loneliness with our thoughts invariably turning to home and to how far we are from family and loved ones. However, the storm and the darkness pass, and what the hell, the adventure is still fun and we are still young (for a while longer anyway), so the gloom is soon forgotten.

The weather finally clears and, late one afternoon, we spot a bright green strip laying on the water directly ahead. It is our first glimpse of Guadalcanal. Suddenly, emergency horns sound the alarm and the loudspeaker blares "Now hear this, general quarters, general quarters, all hands man your battle stations!" Then, as the sailors rush to gun positions and other assigned duties, we look to starboard and see our escort destroyers racing back and forth at great speed, depth charges spewing huge columns of water in their wake.

Quite a show, and we have front row seats. This is our first real submarine alert, letting us know that, if not yet in combat, we are least in the war zone.

However, we seem to be in the way and are soon ordered below, forced to remain in our sweltering troop compartment until the alert is over. Staying below is frustrating as hell as we have the feeling of being very expendable, but the needs of the ship come first. And this feeling of helplessness is not improved one bit by the fact that, during these alerts, all the watertight doors are closed and secured from the outside, leaving us literally imprisoned in our hold. We can do nothing but lay in our bunks and sweat it out. We experience many of these alerts during our rather extended tour, but those occurring at night are the worst. The thin steel side of the ship is seemingly little protection against all that dark water and especially so for those whose bunk is right against the hull. The alert goes on for most of an hour, then the speaker announces, "clear from general quarters, return to standard routine." The watertight doors are opened, and we are once again allowed on deck. Rumor has it that the destroyers sunk a Jap sub but, as usual, we hear nothing official.

The very real threat of Japanese air raids forces us to land after dark on a rather deserted part of the island and, with no docking facilities, we hit the beach in our usual way. The landing is routine, the rough part being that we have to unload all the cargo by landing craft and in the dark to boot. We fight the surf, the sand, and the heavy equipment, working all night without letup as the ships must leave before daylight. Everything must be manhandled on the beach, no matter how heavy or bulky, and I doubt there is any harder work. The dirty job does get done, however, and by daylight.

Guadalcanal is now relatively secure except for air raids and occasional enemy stragglers and, with this new tranquility, has become the main forward base in the South Pacific. We then, being the right folks in the right place at the right time, find ourselves saddled with a variety of tasks. As a matter of fact, our stay is sort of a small adventure in itself. First, a division tent camp is established with you-know-who building the damn thing from scratch. The site is a large coconut grove, which has been completely overgrown with jungle, and we clear it by hand, using machetes and shovels. A back-breaking job, but this is only the first of several we will build as we move up the Pacific.

Next, we get to that which we came for, namely advanced training in jungle warfare. It was a bearcat for the Marines who took this island and, while we hope to learn from their bitter experiences, it doesn't take long to find that there is much misery in the jungle. The heat and humidity are damn near unbearable, not to mention hordes of mosquitoes, flies, and other insects; but the really bad part is that we are destined to fight in a place that is even worse. Ignorance is not such a bad thing.

After spending a couple of hard weeks in this jungle training, our platoon is ordered to outpost duty some miles up the coast. Even though we have been told to expect attacks by Japanese stragglers, this turns out to be a nice break as we get away from camp routine and are able to set up some tents right on the beach. This proves to be a small mistake, how-ever, as we are almost eaten alive by sand fleas the first night. Moving back a ways from the beach seems to help. The mood is more relaxed here, almost like being on vacation, and we take time to swim in the warm Pacific; all the while keeping a sharp eye out for sharks, as this is their kind of country.

One of our assignments is to map as much of the area as possible, and with this in mind, my squad is selected for an overnight patrol into the interior. We have been provided with a native guide, the son of a local chief, and it is his village where we plan to spend the night. Our destination is some miles back in the jungle, and though there is no sign of a trail, our guide apparently sees what we do not, and by late afternoon we arrive at his village. The village is not a large one, perhaps ten or fifteen grass huts, and the chief's "number one Boy," as he calls himself, greets us as we approach. Using gestures and a smattering of pidgin English, we manage to communicate fair-ly well, or at least enough to get by. The menfolk soon drift over to see what's going on, but there is no sign of women or children, and we wonder about that. The chief finally explains that they are in hiding, that there had been bad experiences with the Japanese, and they are therefore fearful of strangers, especially strangers with guns.

However, the chief soon realizes our good inten-tions, and the village relaxes. We are even invited to dinner, the only stipulation being that we shoot one of their chickens for the pot. The chief further insists we use his rifle, a Springfield that he had picked up on one of the battlefields. There is little doubt that the rifle is his pride and joy, but he appears to have some mixed feelings, his pride in owning such a weapon seemingly tempered by a fear that we might take it away. Pride, however, wins and he is beaming as he brings it out of hiding. We let him know that we have no intention of taking his rifle and tell him that he must be a great chief to own such a weapon. He is visibly relieved.

However, after accepting the chief's invitation, we begin to feel concern about losing face should we fail to kill the chicken on the first shot or, worse yet, miss completely, Finally, after determining that only one other and myself shot expert in boot camp, it is decided that he and I flip a coin for the dubious honor. My friend wins the toss, and I am secretly relieved. The entire village is now on hand, and the chief selects a chicken some fifty feet away. Sure that this is a test of sorts, we hope for a clean kill. My buddy takes aim with the chief's rifle, pulls the trigger, and off goes the chicken's head; a perfect shot. The villagers cheer, and we heave a sigh of relief. The chicken is added, along with sweet potatoes and a variety of other local ingredients, to a large pot of water which has been boiling over an open fire while old cannibal movies briefly come to mind. As you might expect, this is not a white-tablecloth affair, and as a matter of fact, there are no tables and not much chicken either, but all in all, dinner is not too bad and has a chicken flavor, anyway.

As we dine, I cannot help but reflect on our adventure and marvel at this screwball war. Here we are, six or seven thousand miles from home, having dinner with a bunch of primitive villagers in the middle of some Godforsaken jungle. The thing seems unreal as hell, as though we have been transported to some other world, and is made even more so by the fact that these folks were headhunters only a few years ago. However, we have learned a thing or two in our short tour of duty, and one of those things is to enjoy what few good things come our way and not look too far ahead. After dinner, our hosts put on a song session, singing church music learned from British missionaries, and the sense of unreality continues. Later, after all the songs have been sung, we are invited to join the men in their local gambling game.

The game, as I remember it, is a bit like craps with sections marked off in the dirt. They have no dice, however, and instead use a variety of objects which are tossed in the air, the winner determined by where they land. To our chagrin, the locals turn out to be sharper than they look, soon relieving us hayseeds of what little money we had and, at the same time, giving us a small lesson in humility. This done, the villagers call it a night and so do we, but not before posting a guard. Japanese stragglers often come to these villages for food, and in addition, we are not totally sure of our host's current status. All goes well, however, and with the benefit of the chief's local knowledge, we complete our map work and head back to the beach.

Our "vacation" ends a day or two later, and we return to the division camp. Back to hard training and regimentation. This return to main camp means we renew our acquaintance with "Washing Machine Charlie," a name given to enemy planes that bomb and torment us most every night and so named because of a rather odd engine sound. "Charlie" usually comes over in groups of two or three, mostly to harass and ruin a good night's sleep; and although the raids don't really do a lot of damage, a few unlucky men are killed and some tents destroyed. The biggest excitement came when he set off Hell's Point ammo dump—what a show!

On a typical night, the air-raid sirens start up around midnight, followed a short time later by "Charlie's" distinctive roar—the worst part is getting woken up and having to run for a bomb shelter. It gets tiresome as hell, which is no doubt what the Japs have in mind. Finally, we get smart enough to dig foxholes alongside our cots, and that helps some, although there are those nights when we just say "to hell with it" and sleep in the damn holes.

Though "Charlie" comes over mostly at night, he occasionally hits us in late afternoon, and it is one of those raids that puts me a bit at risk. Due to the large amount of supplies and equipment arriving by ship, Marine rifle companies are being used as island working parties. To accomplish this, small groups are detached for a couple of weeks and sent to the main ship-loading area, staying in temporary camps near the coast. Without docking facilities, ships have to be offloaded by transferring cargo to barges or landing craft which are then unloaded on the beach. The cargo is then loaded on trucks for its final destination. On this little diversion, we work twelve hours on and twelve off every day, sometimes being assigned to the beach party and sometimes working the ships. The best job, though, is deckhand on the barges, which mainly involves tying and untying the lines that secure them during unloading, and it is an especially good day when that detail comes along. The other jobs are just old-fashioned hard work, however. Our time off is pretty much our own, and that little bit of freedom kind of makes up for the long hours.

This particular day has me working on a newly arrived ship loaded with drums of diesel fuel, gasoline, and assorted oils. It's late afternoon, we already have the mail bags off as they are always first to be unloaded and, in addition, have moved one or two layers of fuel drums down on barges when we notice a group of our patrol planes flying off the port side. Someone comments that the last plane in the group looks different somehow, but with the darkening sky, we really can't be sure. It's not unheard of for a Jap plane to sneak in behind a returning flight, especially around dusk, but we give it no more thought and return to our work. Earlier in the afternoon, we noticed that another ship was being unloaded some miles astern of this one, but with anchored ships being a rather common sight, it was of only passing interest. Suddenly, however, there is a hell of an explosion in the direction of that other ship, and we immediately think of the odd-looking plane—sure now that it was a Jap and sure also that the son of a bitch is probably headed our way.

Others are coming to the same conclusion as the ship's speaker blares, "now hear this, now hear this, enemy aircraft approaching from the stern. Gun crews commence firing as target comes in range, all off-duty crew and working-party personnel clear the ship at once." All of a sudden, we're on our own and waste a few precious seconds deciding what to do. Finally, we just dash to the nearest ladder and make our way topside. Up on deck, we find considerable confusion as there is no time to man lifeboats or even get life jackets. The choice is simple: either jump in the damned ocean or try to shinny down a line to one of the barges—staying on board is not a good option. Most of the barges, however, are partially loaded with drums and are untying as fast as they can, trying to get clear of this possible inferno. We more or less separate at this point, each to find his own solution, and I find myself running along the deck, hoping for some easy way out but not having much luck. I'm thinking that, if the ship is hit, there will probably be one hell of an explosion, sending flaming oil and debris all over the damned place and no doubt setting the ocean on fire as well. It's a kind of damned-if-you-do, damned-if-you-don't thing, and I'm hoping that I don't have to jump, but many are doing just that. So far, however, all the barges have cast off their lines and are backing away when I finally reach the starboard bow and see one with a line still attached. Not being particularly keen about sliding down the thirty or forty feet of line to a barge half-loaded with drums of gasoline, I stand at the rail for a few seconds trying to screw up my courage.

"Hey, Mac," comes a voice from below, "get your ass down if you're coming, cause we're pulling out!" Those were the magic words. I quickly put a leg over the rail, grab the line with both hands and feet, then slide down to the barge. As I hit the deck, the line is released and we begin slowly backing away. I can see the Jap plane now, flying low and coming in fast from the stern. Time seems to stop as we watch in a kind of horrible fascination, unable or perhaps unwilling to believe this is really happening. The plane passes over the bow just as the front section of the ship explodes. Our barge is perhaps fifty or sixty feet away as flaming oil and debris begin falling around us, and we start to feel some serious concern due to our dangerous cargo. There is even talk of trying to push the damn barrels off but, in the end, there just isn't time, and we set about helping those in the water.

Explosions continue to light the sky as flames make their way into other parts of the ship, and with burning oil now spreading over large patches of ocean, those who had chosen to or were forced to jump are trying to get the hell out of the way. Oncoming darkness only adds to the problem as barges and other craft move around picking up survivors while, at the same time, trying to stay clear of the flames. Not really a fun evening, but eventually all are picked up, at least all who could be found. I assume some are lost this night but never do hear how many. It is just one rather small incident in this war, yet it seems that we are drawing ever closer to the hell.

Sneaking in behind a flight of our patrol planes, that enemy pilot was able to sink two of our ships in just a matter of minutes and, due to the late hour and the suddenness of his attack, get away with hardly a shot being fired. Not bad for an afternoon's work. He'll certainly be a hero in Japan, no doubt get a medal from the Emperor, and I imagine the bastard is, by now, thanking his particular god and drinking a toast to his successful mission. To us, however, he is merely a dirty, no-good son of a bitch. It all depends on where you're sitting.

A short time after this little incident, I manage to celebrate my nineteenth birthday. This past year has been interesting, but the real hell of it is that the next ones are going to be even more than interesting as our education is extended into the finer points of misery and fear. To say that it is a blessing to not be permitted to look into the future is somewhat of an understatement.

Getting back to our detached status here on the beach, the camp's proximity to many supply dumps gives us an opportunity to engage in one of the basic rules of Marine Corps life. Marines are, by nature, scroungers. We seem to be last on every list except one (you know the one). "Simulate" is standard procedure and "make do" a second motto. Unfortunately, this lack of things that others often consider necessities, along with a feeling of always being on the short end, encourages the requisition of items which, some would say, do not really belong to us. In addition, and almost if by plan, this is a time of nightly air raids and we are further helped by the fact that, on these occasions, the guards of these supply dumps head for the bomb shelters.

So, considering our heritage, this favorable combination of events is just too good to pass up, and we consider it our duty to make the most of it. Off the record, of course, this is how I came to be "issued" my Navy (diver's) knife, it being the handiest of tools and the one I have with me at all times. Another indispensable item on these forays, as well as on work details in supply dumps, especially Army dumps (they are the best), is a spoon. So, never knowing when fortune might decide to smile, we try never to be without these two items.

In due course, we become quite adept at selecting things which either taste good or serve a particular need. However, even our experienced noses fail us on occasion. On one of these, we appropriate an especially beautiful and quite heavy wooden box, sure that it must contain something of value and would add to the quality of our lives. Instead, the thing turns out to be one of our few real failures and a bitter disappointment. Those who plan these things must have decided to play a joke, for they packed this lovely box with bars of soap. Having carried this heavy thing some distance, our anger is considerable. We also feel there should be some sort of rules—after all, fair is fair.

Finally, as our tour of duty as the island working party is winding down, we get sidetracked for one more little task, namely loading bombs on B-24 Liberators. The campaign for the New Georgia Islands, just north of Guadalcanal, is in full swing with bombers taking off and landing in a steady stream. This being a bit more activity than the ground crews can handle, we are asked to help out. The big push lasts only a few days, but we add yet another to our ever-growing list of skills, skills that no doubt will come in handy after the war.

That chore finally completed, we get back to intense training and all the little comforts that go with infantry life in the field. Hard and tiresome but hopefully worth it when we get to the nitty-gritty of real combat. I constantly wonder when it will be.

Shortly after our return to main camp, a boot camp buddy from the Raiders looked me up. He had just returned from the New Georgia fighting, and he wasted little time giving me the lowdown on this combat business. Even though suspecting that the thing was no picnic, I was still surprised by his rather strong description of all the misery and especially the fear. However, I figured (maybe hoped is the word) that he was just laying it on a bit to impress an old buddy. After my first dose of real terror a month or so later, I finally understood what he had been trying to tell me. The hell of it is, my buddy understated the thing by at least a country mile.

Air raids continue most every night, but it is a rarity when an enemy plane is shot down. We often watch as the searchlights catch our visitors in their beams and anti-aircraft batteries fire hundreds of rounds into the sky, but seldom do we see any hits. Finally, on a night in early October, the lights pick up two Jap planes coming to visit, and this time it is different. Instead of the usual ack-ack all over the sky, another plane flashes through the lights, and in a matter of minutes both enemy planes are shot down. Men all over the island roar with glee, somehow sensing that the tide may finally be turning. The American plane is one of our new night fighters and a sign of the changes coming in the South Pacific. It will soon change even more, and we will be part of that change.

BOUGAINVILLE

The first one will be looked forward to.

October 1943

O ctober brings increased activity, and once again, a new excitement is in the air. Rumors are everywhere, which in this crazy outfit could mean that anything or nothing is about to happen. In this case, however, it turns out to be a definite something, and around the middle of the month the rumors are confirmed. The Ninth Marines, Third Marine Division, Fleet Marine Force in the field, is going to hit the Japs. There is only exhilaration and thoughts of high adventure as we pack seabags for storage and prepare for a combat operation. We are ready, even eager, to get going and besides, we're damned tired of incessant training and itching to give the Japs some hell.

However, I must mention that this is not the first time our division has been ordered to prepare for battle.

As a matter of fact, we were on the verge of boarding ship a couple of times only to be left with that let-down feeling when the landings were called off. So, with these "disappointments" in mind, the battalion commander felt a small joke might be to put our present situation in proper context. The story, as I remember it, takes place on a small naval vessel and it has to do with a quite regular function of ships at sea: namely, fire drills. On this particular ship, these drills invariably centered around the galley, and the routine was always the same. The captain, when the mood took him, would call down on the intercom and instruct the cook to sound the alarm. The cook, who it must be noted spoke with a distinct Cuban accent, would then get on the horn and yell, "Fire in the galley! Fire in the galley!" bringing the fire detail on the run. This, unfortunately, became quite routine over time, accompanied by a noticeable lessening of enthusiasm on the part of the crew.

Finally, as these things are wont to do, a fire really did break out in the galley, and the cook immediately got on the horn yelling "Fire in the galley! Fire in the galley!" Then, remembering the rather lackadaisical efforts of the past, he quickly added this brief note: "No sheet this time!"

At last, then, with preparations finally complete, we don helmets, packs, and cartridge belts—then grab our rifles and march to the coast, leaving our comfortable tents for God knows what. At the beach, we wade the few yards to our waiting Higgins boat, then proceed to our ship, the USS *Crescent City*. We board in our usual manner by climbing up the nets and then head down to our assigned troop compartment. As usual, it is crowded and hot as hell, but we eventually locate bunks, get our gear off, and begin to feel at home. "Home," as the saying goes, "is where you hang your helmet."

Then, with our heavy equipment and supplies having already been loaded, the various ships set conditions for sea and the convoy immediately gets underway. We, of course, have been trying to figure out where in the hell we're going, and as we clear Guadalcanal, the suspense is finally lifted. Our destination, we are now informed, is Bougainville: the largest and northernmost of the Solomon Islands. The plan is for a surprise landing on November 1, and my platoon is one of those sharing the dubious honor of landing in the first wave. They tell us this island is similar to Guadalcanal, only bigger, with a great probability of more swamps and denser jungle, and an additional bit of good news is that we land in one of the swampiest areas. It is getting closer, whatever it is that awaits.

However, with the plan calling for a practice landing on the island of Efate in the New Hebrides, our initial heading is south. At this point, we are issued our supply of ammo along with rations for three days and a warning that they might have to last longer The US Navy is still not able to come and go as it pleases in these waters.

Our food consists of "C" rations, which are small cans of stew, hash, or meat and beans plus a can of hard crackers for breakfast and dinner, with a concentrated chocolate bar called "D" rations intended for lunch. Riflemen are issued ten eight-round clips of ammo for cartridge belts plus a bandoleer containing a half-dozen more clips. In addition, we are issued four hand grenades. The grenades are a particular problem as the damned things don't seem to fit anywhere. So, with this in mind, the good ladies of New Zealand knitted shoulder bags for us and, though not the perfect solution, it seemed better than stuffing them in our pockets. We wear a field pack, carry two canteens, first-aid kit, poncho, knife, and entrenching tool as well as our M1 rifle and bayonet. In addition, the poor old assistant BAR men, like myself, wear a belt around our chest containing twelve twenty-round magazines for the automatic rifle. Carrying anywhere from seventy-five to over a hundred pounds each, we wonder about fighting in all this gear and decide that it is going to be one hell of a war.

Our practice landing goes reasonably well and, as usual, is mostly a lot of hard work for the infantry. Then, with that little chore out of the way, the convoy once again puts to sea, and this time, the heading is north. Make-believe is over, and we are anxious to get on with the adventure. But there is something odd about it all as we steam along with destroyer escorts on our flanks. Although the convoy has this warlike appearance, there is a strange, deceptive calm on board, and we have trouble grasping the fact that our regiment really is going into combat and that some of us will be killed. The first one and the bliss of ignorance, I suppose. This, you may be sure, will not be a problem on future voyages.

Unfortunately or no (depending on one's discomfort level), it is to be our lot to suffer more than a passing acquaintance with troop transports and convoys. However, we find that there is a certain uniformity to this life at sea once you get the hang of it. And with the war stretching over vast areas of ocean, we, and especially those of us who stick around awhile, are destined to get the hang of it. Abandon-ship drills are but one of the routines, and we can always count on at least one every day. These things usually begin with the duty officer determining a time which is most likely to irritate the greatest number—at least that's the way it seems to us. Then he sounds "general quarters," explaining that, "this is a drill." At that time, the emergency horns wail their urgent message, sailors rush to battle stations, and troops report to designated abandon-ship locations. This is always accompanied by much griping and cursing, as we are required to bundle up in heavy kapok life jackets. The drills usually last a half hour or so, and that is more than enough as we stand in close formation, trying to keep our balance on the moving deck. Once in a while, however, the Navy uses this opportunity for gunnery practice and in so doing, puts on a show of sorts. This is done by having aircraft tow a sleeve (target) alongside the convoy while the various gunners take their turn at it. A lot of fireworks, cheers from the crew when their ship scores a hit, and a bit of a diversion for the troops.

Now, with D-Day getting closer by the hour, we spend much of our time on refresher courses in compass reading, signaling, and the multitude of subjects that relate to our survival. Weapons, of course, are checked and rechecked while combat packs and other gear are made ready. Individual and squad assignments are gone over time and again, and in between, we are detailed to various tasks such as cleaning troop compartments and heads, as well as occasional KP duty. The galley, in particular, is miserably hot, and most of us wind up with heat rash on that detail. The only saving thing is being able to swipe an extra orange or apple, and that almost makes up for the misery.

Then, a day or two before D-Day, a different kind of misery arrives for me as I get something in my eye. Very painful and the damned thing doesn't go away. My buddies tell me to go see the doc, but I am afraid they won't let me make the landing. However, the discomfort finally becomes so intense that I can put it off no longer and reluctantly head for sick bay. A corpsman puts a soothing something in my eye and removes a tiny piece of steel. Blessed relief, and most importantly, I am allowed to hit the beach with my squad.

Evening is a time to relax as some play cards or read while others lean against the rail, watching the water rush by as they shoot the breeze with buddies and think of home. Home seems farther away all the time and now, for the first time, we seriously wonder if we are ever to see our families again.

Down here, night comes quickly with the setting sun leaving the convoy in a sort of gloomy darkness. On moonlit nights, however, nearby ships are quite visible as they cut silently through the seas, taking us to whatever in hell it is that fate has in store. Now, on this, our last evening by the rail, our last night to sack out in a bunk, we linger somewhat longer than usual—each talking to God in his own way, each hoping for some small assurance that all will go well tomorrow. Although some seem to find that which they seek, most will hit the beach their questions unanswered.

November 1, 1943

"General quarters" is sounded at first light, and the crew begins final preparations for debarking troops while our Island and our adventure get closer by the minute. Secured down in our troop compartment, we cannot see the activity on deck, however, we can hear the various commands coming over loudspeakers and so have a pretty good idea of what is taking place top-side. Now, quite suddenly, the small emergency lights are turned off, leaving our compartment in total dark-ness, and adding yet another to our already long list of things to gripe about. In addition, it is stiflingly hot, seemingly even more so than usual, and there is noth-ing to do but lay on our bunks while we wait for the orders that will send us on our way. Saying that we are impatient to get out of this Goddamned hold is but another large understatement.

The speaker is busy now as crew members race to complete last-minute chores, and we note that time is winding down. "Now hear this, lower all boats to the rail." It won't be long now, as winches move Higgins boats from positions on deck and in davits to railside where they will be held until the ship drops anchor. Though we hear and sense the activity around us, it does not really sink in that this tremendous effort is merely to land a few Marines on an unknown beach in the middle of nowhere. This with the hope that they can overcome an enemy who is equally determined. Then, with a rather unexpected finality, the anchor chain rattles down the side of the ship, and the loudspeaker immediately commands, "Lower all boats to the water." We are here!

Hatch covers are now opened over cargo holds while landing nets are dropped over the side and winches complete the task of lowering the various landing craft into the water. No time is wasted as all are well aware that the Japanese will hit us hard as soon as they can. Laying in the darkness, waiting for the words that will forever change our lives, we begin to feel the first faint stirring of apprehension.

Could it be that the adventure will not be what we think?

Then in a sudden blast of the speaker, apprehension is forgotten. "Now hear this—Marines assigned to the first trip of boats, prepare to disembark." That's us! It's a son of a bitch as we struggle into packs and other gear, in total darkness, no less. There just isn't room for all of us in the narrow passageways, resulting in much confusion, bumping, and cursing. However, and in spite of it all, we somehow manage to get ready.

Finally, in one more blast of the speaker, the words we have been waiting for: "Now hear this, now hear this, Marines landing in the first wave, report to your debarkation stations." This is it! Rebel yells and rowdy cheers almost drown out the sergeant. "You bastards think you want to fight, then move out." Battling the dark and the confusion, we stumble into some kind or order, all the while cursing a blue streak as we climb the ladders and move out on deck. Taking only brief note of the beautiful Solomon Islands morning, we eagerly take that first breath of fresh air, the cool ocean breeze a blessed relief after that stinking troop compartment.

There is much activity on deck as other units join us, all heading for pre-assigned debarking stations. Our net is located at the port bow, and we get our first look at Bougainville as we approach railside. Dark green with mountains inland, the son of a bitch looks big and, in the early morning light, forbidding. What kind of terror lies hidden in all that green? We are soon to find out, though it is still hard for us to get it through our thick skulls that this is the real thing. That misery and death actually wait. It still seems like just another practice landing with all hands back aboard ship tonight.

However, a semblance of reality begins to sink in as destroyers open fire on enemy positions and aircraft zoom in to strafe the beaches. Caught now in this strange kind of limbo, we watch the goings-on and wait for the words that will send us down the nets. Landing craft are now on station below, and we listen to that old familiar sound as coxswains gun their engines, moving the boats forward and back in an effort to stay in position. Finally, all that is left is to wait out that little lull before the storm is unleased.

Standing by the rail, we take these last minutes to recheck our gear, making sure our heavy load is set for the climb down. This means helmet straps unbuckled, rifles slung on left shoulders with slings hung over bayonet handles (attached to packs), and left side canteens pulled through slings at butts. Cartridge belts have been hooked to packs and left hanging open in front. All this to get rid of the stuff quickly in the event one should suddenly find himself in the ocean instead of the boat. In addition (as if we needed any more Goddamned crap hanging on us), we wear bulky life belts around our waists. And, as usual, the damn things had to be blown up by mouth, the promised CO_2 cartridges failing (again) to arrive.

Nevertheless, we are ready as can be. Ready for what, I wish I knew. These small doubts aside, we are anxious, even eager to go, to get this whatever-it-is under our belts. The sudden sound of the speaker jars our reverie. "Now hear this," is followed by another voice with a British accent: "This is the captain speaking." He gives a short speech, reminding us of how important it is that we knock hell out of the bastards. Then he wishes us good luck and a speedy victory, this with a recording of the Marine Hymn in the background. He concludes with the classic phrase, "Land the Landing Force." God help us now!

Over the rail and down we go, struggling to find footholds in the ratty old net. One might think they would have enough common decency to put out good ones for special occasions like this, but so much for wishful thinking and decency. Considering the weight we carry and the lousy net, it's a wonder none of us fall; however, all goes well and in a matter of minutes, we are in the boat. The net is then tossed over the side, the coxswain guns the engine, and we are away.

H-hour on Bougainville. The ship's captain blared the Marine's hymn over the loudspeaker as we climbed down the nets.

No fear yet, just exhilaration and a sense of adventure as we head for a rendezvous with the eight or nine others in our boat group. At that point, the boats form up in a circular pattern which will be maintained until word is received to begin the invasion. Packed in like sardines, it is uncomfortable as hell and no help that the sea begins to get choppy from constant circling. Now, as H-hour approaches, most of us wonder what it will be like, wonder if we will even make it to the beach and, deep down, wonder if we will be up to it. As we look for answers, the ship suddenly flashes a signal to the coxswain, and we begin to pick up speed. Soon, boat groups all along the line move out of their circular patterns into ragged *V* formations and head toward the beach. The show is about to begin.

Some distance ahead, we see the "line of departure," consisting of a lone picket boat standing two or three miles offshore and in communication with the command ship. Once past this so-called line, there is no turning back. Another signal now and the boats in the rear part of the *V*s increase speed and begin to pull up even with the lead boats. Then, as they catch up and form a sort of irregular line, the coxswains increase throttle, the idea being to reach top speed by the time we hit the line of departure.

At this point, we begin to see flashes of gunfire coming from the island followed by explosions in and around the boats. The Japs are shooting back, and a few unlucky landing craft are hit. It is just about now that the thought hits us, and we ask ourselves, "what in the Goddamned hell are we doing in this stinking boat, in this miserable Godforsaken place, about to get our ass shot off?" Too late to worry about it now, we are in the Goddamned war.

• • • • • •

The picket boat flashes a go signal, our landing craft passes the line of departure at near full speed, and we are guaranteed a closeup look at hell. For our protection, they say, we are ordered to crouch down below the gunwales. In reality, it is just another of the small miseries that we are not allowed to see this hell we are heading into. The sergeant calls out, "Lock and load, then unlock." We slip the safety on, pull back the bolt of our M1, insert an eight-round clip, and slam the bolt forward, forcing a cartridge into the chamber. The safety is then pushed off and it is all for real. "Fix bayonets" comes next and, with these two words, the thing is personal and immediate.

This being our first combat landing, there is plenty of wisecracking and rough humor, though many use these last few minutes for private thoughts and prayer. In the back of all our minds, however, is one nagging thought, and that is: what will happen when that ramp goes down? The sergeant calls out, "Five hundred yards to go," and the old Lewis machine guns mounted on the boat open fire. These are manned by members of our platoon, giving them the distinction of being first to fire against the enemy. "One hundred yards now, brace yourselves." We hold onto each other and any part of the boat within reach. We have been told a thousand times and are told once more: "When you hit the beach, spread out and keep moving." Time has just about run out, but we hardly notice. "Fifty yards," then *crash*! We are tumbled into each other as the boat hits a sand bar. The coxswain drops the front ramp, too soon, we think, and we are immediately ordered to "move out!"

As ordered, we jump off the ramp, the weight of our gear taking us completely under. "Son of a no-good bitch!" What a way to start a war, soaking wet and especially our rifles, all so carefully cleaned. Cursing the coxswain and our luck, we struggle to get footing as the waves slam against us. We can hear machine-gun fire and explosions as we slosh through the last few yards of surf but can't see a damn thing. Finally free of the sea, we cross a narrow strip of beach and begin hacking our way through an almost solid wall of jungle. There is no time to reflect that we were first to hit the beach or, for that matter, that we are still alive. We push through as fast as possible; the Goddamned brush so thick we have to use machetes and knives to make any headway. I haven't personally seen any Japs yet, but I understand some have seen too many and are having a hell of a time getting through strong defenses. Just the luck of the draw, I guess; and without a doubt, we will have our fill of them before this is over.

"What in the Goddamned hell?" All of a sudden the air is filled with the terrifying sound of engines roaring down from above, then the sharp crackle of machine-gun fire. Can't see the sky because of dense growth, but the Jap air force must have found us out, and they are giving us an appropriate welcome. The sound is incredible, no doubt magnified by the jungle, and seems to be everywhere. There is no place to hide, just hit the ground, curl up, and make as small a target as possible. No time even to dig in, time only to pray. It is only the first of many times that I will pray in desperation, and it comes surprisingly easy. Facing real terror for the first time, we literally have the living hell scared out of us and quickly decide that this thing is for real, that a guy could easily get killed in a place like this. The raid lasts twenty or thirty minutes but seemed like it would never end. Thanks, God.

Exhilaration is somehow slipping away, and we begin to have the first doubts about our adventure. Up to now, at least, we have faced only light resistance but are already beat, our camouflaged dungarees soaked with sweat and, in addition, are finding that our other enemy, the jungle, is a formidable one. Throw in a few stinking swamps and it is a son of a bitch just maintaining contact with units on our flanks. As if that isn't enough, we disturb hordes of hungry (starving is more like it) mosquitoes as we are initiated into the gentle art of jungle warfare and the hell of it is that it is not going to get any better. However, our first day in action finally ends with orders to dig in for the night. It won't be the longest or the hardest—only the first.

Most take their entrenching tools and start digging. A few "lucky" ones, like myself, are ordered back to the beach for ammo and water. Not being overly happy to begin with, we are even less so when we find that all the ships have gone, and then our morale drops even further when we notice that the beaches are strewn with damaged Higgins boats. What the hell happened? Did the Navy get their asses whipped? We quickly recall the difficult situation other Marines faced in the early days of the Guadalcanal campaign and wonder if we too will be left to fend for ourselves.

Not until later do we learn of the big naval and air battle that forced our transports to seek safer waters. In reality, the US Navy kicked the hell out of the Japs and, unbeknown to us, the ships will return in the morning. As for the Higgins boats, many were damaged by Japanese artillery fire and strafing aircraft, the rest by a vicious tide and difficult beach. From our small view, however, things look bad, and it is a rather discouraged group that heads back to the lines.

It is almost dark, and we are bushed by the time we get "home" only to be reminded that there are still foxholes to be dug. To make the day a real winner, I have a miserable headache and heave my guts out as I shovel. Haven't found the glory yet; maybe it comes later.

Two long miserable months will pass before we again walk the decks of our troop transports and, by that time, the old scows will undoubtedly look like the Taj Mahal. Although it hadn't sunk in before, we are finally beginning to accept the fact that some of us are destined to stay here. The problem is, we don't know who. Perhaps it is just as well left that way, though we will find it increasingly difficult to keep those thoughts out of mind.

As we go about this sometimes-bloody business, fear and exhaustion are to be constant companions, and we will have more than a passing acquaintance with malaria, tropical ulcers, dysentery, and jungle rot as well as assorted other miseries. Hunger and thirst go almost without saying. I hesitate to even mention rain, mud, steep mountains, swamp, and of course, the jungle. More appropriately, the miserable, stinking, terrifying jungle. In addition, our enemy is cruel and determined, rarely seen, and fights to the bitter end. It is also sad but true that we are destined to spend almost the entire campaign on or in front of the lines, and so will not have the luxury of even a single second to relax. So much for the bad part, the good part is, well, I hate to say it, but we never found the good part. Maybe the ones lost in these first battles are lucky, how horrible to go through all this hell and be struck down in the last one.

Getting back to the business at hand, the next night finds me delving a bit further into this thing called fear as another and myself are selected for outpost duty. Selected for hell is more like it as we will be stuck a hundred yards or so in front of the lines, to be the first hit if the Japs attack. This, however, being your basic no-questions-asked, do-as-you're-damn-well-told kind of outfit, we just grab our rifles and, after a small wistful look at our buddies, head out with the squad leader as ordered. He selects a suitable spot just before dark and then, kind soul that he is, leaves a few extra grenades along with an admonition about being Goddamned sure one of us stays awake. At this point we mention, although it could have sounded like a complaint, that if the Japs hit us, we really will be up that well-known creek and without a paddle. He more or less agrees but adds the small consolation that if the bastards do attack, we can, after being sure the lines have been alerted, then figure we did our duty and get the hell out. He was, however, a bit evasive when it came to the how and where part.

That bit of kindness ends the good news, and as our squad leader takes his leave, daylight fades, and with that, the jungle seems to close in around us. For those who have somehow missed this dubious pleasure, the jungle at night *is* intimidating, to say the least, and is especially so for a couple of barely-dry-behind-the-ears nineteen-year-olds. However, to make a long story and an even longer, more miserable night short, the Japs choose not to hit our little outpost that night, but it is still a scary son of a bitch.

Though this campaign has some large engagements, a good deal of the fighting takes place in small skirmishes or on patrol. The damn patrols especially are a son of a bitch, and the constant threat of ambush, snipers, and booby traps puts them near the bottom of our list of fun things to do. Nevertheless, they are just one of many nasty but necessary parts of this business, and each squad has to take its turn. To reduce the chance of ambush, we take one compass course going out and always return on a different one. Keeping these headings, however, is much easier said than done, as we must constantly go around and over obstacles while, at the same time, keeping a sharp eye out for the enemy. Maddening, that's what it is as we try to look everywhere at once.

The jungle, at times, is so dense that we have to hold on to each other or risk being separated. Deep swamps are another delight, and we spend many hours in the slimy, foul-smelling things. Rarely able to touch bottom, we try to keep our balance while stepping from one fallen limb to another and not always succeeding. In addition, the bushes crawl with a multitude of insects, all seemingly eager to swarm over any warm body that comes near.

Leeches, snakes, and God knows what else attack under water while mosquitoes and flies control the air. It is always a relief just to get back to the good old front lines, even though it's sometimes short lived.

During a return from one of these early patrols, we take our first and only prisoner while at the same time getting a close-up look at our seldom-seen enemy. We find the poor devil lying in a small jungle clearing, apparently quite sick and no doubt left to die by his comrades—perhaps we were getting too close. Seemingly little more than a bag of bones, yet he is the enemy and would no doubt, if given the chance, kill us without remorse. However, it is now us who have that choice with at least half the patrol ready to kill the son of a bitch on the spot and the others opting for mercy either out of compassion or a hope that he may be of some use to intelligence. I don't know why, but I was one of those leaning toward life, as was the patrol leader, although perhaps for different reasons. So, miserable-looking creature that he was, we finally decided to let him live and, under protest from some, carried the poor bastard back to headquarters. Although we have been at this for only a few days, I am already discovering how easy it is to take that first step back and then finding that, once the first one has been taken, the next ones are easier still.

Misery is but one part of this business; death and injury are another as we all lose buddies to these God-damned patrols. Among those lost is my best friend, killed on patrol during the second week, and everything seems to change after that. The war is getting meaner, and it becomes more and more apparent that, if we are to keep our sanity in all this hell, we must build some kind of barrier to keep out the hurt. Those who do not often break under the strain, while those who do frequently build their wall too damn thick.

As disagreeable as the days are in this miserable jungle war, nightfall brings a special kind of terror. We are fond of saying, "the days are hell, but oh, the nights," and if anything, the son of a bitch is an understatement. Darkness comes suddenly and is often preceded by late afternoon rain, which means we start out soaked and then spend the rest of the night in a muddy hole, sometimes lying in several inches of water to boot. If we ever get our hands on the son of a bitch who organized this tour!

To compound our misery, the Japs attempt to infiltrate our lines under the cover of darkness, forcing us to use two-man foxholes with one man always awake. Quite innocently, we start the campaign with four-hour watches, but it isn't long before the reality of moving up all day and little sleep forces us into one-hour stints. Then, even that one hour eventually becomes unbearable but, having no alternative, we just tough it out.

Finally, as the bitter days turn to weeks and even months, an overpowering exhaustion sets in, and the miserable battle to stay awake becomes a kind of exquisite torture followed then by frustration as we find it almost impossible to relax when we do get our turn to sleep. Making the thing especially difficult is the fact that we must lie on our backs, instantly ready to fight off an attacker yet barely able to move for fear of giving away our position. Adding to the general discomfort, our foxholes are never any bigger than necessary, as we seem to be digging a new one damn near every night. The danger, though, is real and the penalty for carelessness severe, as many are killed in these lonely encounters. The Japanese also die at night, but we feel this is what it is all about and consider their demise good riddance. We are learning, however, not to take this enemy of ours too lightly. He may be a dirty, no-good son of a bitch, but he is tough and does not give up.

Distinguishing between friend and foe at night is another Goddamned misery and one that we try to overcome by staying in our foxholes, assuming that any movement above ground is the enemy. Although these self-imposed rules help us survive, they do bring unexpected difficulties. For example, if you must relieve yourself at night, you do what you must do in your foxhole—being careful of your buddy, of course.

Which reminds me of steel helmets, the heavy old "pots" having, as a complete surprise to all, turned out to be rather handy. Issued mainly for protection, the damned things wind up being used as shovels, chairs, pillows, cook pots, wash basins, and heads (latrines). A nuisance when you don't need the miserable things, worth their weight in gold when you do, and if we didn't have them, we'd probably have to invent the damn things.

There is something else about this jungle at night and that is the Godawful racket. The place is a veritable bedlam of sound as birds, animals, and insects add their distinctive voices to the general uproar. However, we soon learn that not all these sounds are genuine as others take advantage of the clamor, trying to imitate certain ones as a form of communication. Although our enemy has a number of these in his repertoire, a particular favorite resembles two sticks being hit together, and it is damn hard to tell the real from the fake.

Getting back to the "chorus," the damn thing may go on for some time and then stop suddenly, as though some unseen director is at work. For us, however, laying in our muddy foxhole, the abrupt and always unexpected silence means only one thing: that our enemy is moving about and that the son of a bitch is perhaps a bit too close for comfort. Unfortunately, that is a real possibility, and the thought of a knife or grenade in the dark sends a distinct chill down our spines.

On other occasions, the lull is merely some unknown jungle whimsy, but whatever the cause, our raggedy chorus eventually starts up again, and when it does, the routine is always the same. First, a few hesitant sounds and then, as more and more join in, the beat slowly builds back to the previous clatter. Finally, as the hubbub returns to what is considered normal around here, it brings with it a strange sense of relief, as though our jungle world is once again saying all is well and, for the moment, that is enough. However, the miserable hell of it is that this brief bit of comfort rarely lasts and, instead, is all too soon replaced by fear.

Although many nights are so pitch black that we literally cannot see our hand in front of our face, there are those that have just enough light to make out shadowy forms such as trees and bushes. If we look long enough, however, these objects often appear to move and even take on human-like shapes. Sometimes, of course, the shapes really are human, and that is the frustrating part, not knowing which is the plain old tree. It becomes a deadly sort of game as we try to keep the enemy from locating our position, and he uses whatever means he can think of to find us. He even resorts to taunts, using phrases like "Marine, you die" or "Roosevelt is a son of a bitch, ha, ha, ha," thinking these insults would make us mad enough to respond. It seemed to bother them when, on occasion, we would curse the emperor, and they just cannot understand that we don't give a good Goddamn what they say about Roosevelt or even Eleanor. As a matter of fact, we curse the old man pretty regularly ourselves.

Anyway, we have learned the hard way to keep our cool and have a standing order about firing at night unless under direct attack. Our only recourse, if we get irritated enough or think he is close enough, is to toss a grenade, but the damn things have a particularly nasty habit of hitting something and bouncing back, so we think twice about even that response. Like it or not, with the rules of this nighttime game being what they are, we have to stay put and let the Jap come to us.

Then, in addition to the aforementioned small unpleasantries, artillery and mortar fire tear at our already ragged nerves. Sometimes just close enough to scare the hell out of us and ruin what little chance we get at sleep, while others the miserable stuff is close in and deadly. Try as I may, I cannot find words to describe the gut-wrenching fear, the never knowing where the sons of bitches are going to hit, or the terrible uncertainty of surviving even the next second. In addition, friendly fire occasionally drops in and, without a doubt, our own is worst of all. It is, however, just one of the many hard truths in this hellish business that close-in support has a price, and that price is the occasional short round. Perhaps then, with these and various other nighttime delights (son of a bitch, almost forgot the Goddamn mosquitoes), one might understand and even sympathize with our silent plea for an early dawn. The day will no doubt bring its share of misery; it's just that the horrors seem not quite so horrible in daylight.

There is little escape from the agony—moving up, patrolling, or attacking by day, then terror at night. For the "lucky" survivors, the days turn into weeks, then the weeks become months. We have, by now, lost track of the day as well as the date and no longer care. For the most part, however, we do what has to be done and little more, then gripe like hell about everything. Fortunately, we are provided with ample opportunity to avail ourselves of this little safety valve, and I doubt we could keep our sanity without it.

Finally, after almost a month on the front lines, we are ordered into reserve and move a hundred yards or so to the rear. Reserve. God, what a feeling. Even though we must still maintain normal security, especially at night, there is something about just being off the line and, for a short while at least, getting away from the constant misery. However, while digging in for the night, I am bit, twice yet, by a damned scorpion, and it hurts like hell. Hope things get better.

In the morning, we crawl out of our foxholes with the sun, as usual, and get a pleasant surprise. They tell us it is Thanksgiving, or close to it, and best of all, the president has ordered that all troops are to at least have a shot at a turkey dinner. We can hardly believe they really mean poor devils like us, way back in the boondocks as we are, but damn if the cooks haven't somehow wrestled cooking equipment up the steep trails. Nothing fancy, just some fifty-gallon fuel drums which have been cut in half, but it isn't long before fires are lit and an almost forgotten aroma fills the air. Roast turkey it isn't, canned turkey and stew it is. Not like home, but what the hell. Besides, we haven't been dining too well lately, and as a matter of fact, this will be our first real meal since—hell, I can't even remember our last good meal. In reserve and now this, maybe our luck is changing.

We have almost forgotten how to react to pleasant surprises, but noontime finds us in the chow line, smiling for a change. As some, however—and there are those who tend to look on the dark side—might have expected, a small fly is seen crawling in the ointment. Rain starts coming down hard, and before long, our stew has turned into soup. So what, just a minor change in the menu; although, in truth, there was a complaint or two.

Soaking wet by now, rain pouring off my helmet, I get my serving and plop down in the mud to share Thanksgiving dinner with buddies. As usual, we gripe about these somewhat-less-than-ideal dining arrangements, while at the same time trying to make the most of our good fortune. You know how it is, give a guy a break and all of a sudden, he wants conditions. I take a few bites and think back to another time, wondering about my family. Perhaps they are also sitting down to dinner. I can just picture it, turkey surrounded by all the trimmings, no doubt on a clean white tablecloth with everyone talking and having a good time. I wonder if they think of—"Attention, Second Platoon, we're movin' out! Forget the Goddamned turkey and get your asses in gear!" Dirty, no-good, rotten son of a bitch, can't we get a break just once?

Miserable, Goddamn bastards! We hurriedly throw out our holiday dinner, clean our mess kits, then get the rest of our gear together and fall into formation heading for God knows what. As we move out, the sergeant tells us we have been ordered to push on to the other side of the division perimeter, a distance of some miles, then attack an enemy strongpoint first thing in the morning. Because we have to be in position tonight, this will be a forced march through some of the most Godawful country in the world, and he ends on the happy note that stragglers will not be tolerated. Our lovely Thanksgiving is fast going to hell, though we probably should have known it was just too good to be true. That, by the way, was the end of our stay in reserve, and there will be no more in this campaign.

The hours go by with no stopping and no rest as we constantly struggle to keep up. At times, the mud is so thick that it takes all our strength just to pull one leg up, only to plop it down and then have to do the same with the other. "Wait-a-minute vines" tear our clothes and skin, their thorns so sharp and the vines so strong that we are forced to stop and disentangle ourselves—hence the name "wait a minute." In addition, the difficulty of keeping our footing on muddy slopes along with the constant battering of the jungle eventually brings on an almost unbearable exhaustion. Still, we somehow keep going, taking one step at a time, although we finally reach that point where there is almost nothing left. The struggle has become no more than the will to continue putting one foot out in front of the other. No one asks how much longer or how much farther; we only try to force our legs to take that next step. A few get sick after "gorging" themselves on holiday fare and then being forced into this little stroll through the woods. Those with pain they cannot stand fall by the wayside and are left to their misery. Threats of dire consequences mean nothing as they are beyond caring. To their credit, all eventually catch up and are on hand for tomorrow's activities. The rain continues without letup, mercifully hiding the fact that we must relieve ourselves as we trudge along.

Dirty, no-good, son-of-a-bitching Goddamn war. Dirty, no-good, son-of-a-bitching Goddamn bastardly jungle. Dirty, no-good, son-of-a-bitching Goddamn bastardly, stinking mud. These thoughts and others like them continually run through our minds as we are too Goddamn beat even to curse out loud. Everything and everyone even remotely connected with the war and our misery gets its share of attention—then we start over again. Finally, the agony becomes so intense that we wonder if it is worth going on. Death may be waiting tomorrow, or some other day, so why go through this torture? What in the Goddamned hell keeps us going? Esprit de corps, damned if I know.

Then, just as it is turning dark, we find ourselves on the slope of a fairly steep hill and are ordered to dig in for the night. Thank God for small favors! Time is taken to gulp down some cold hash or stew, but most of us are too exhausted to eat more than a few bites and use our remaining strength to scoop out minimal foxholes. Other Marines, occupying the line above us, have taken many casualties trying to dislodge the Japs from well-dug-in positions a couple hundred yards in front. It will be our turn in the morning. Not a pleasant thought this night, and we wonder, as we have on other nights, about our chances tomorrow. Prayer and hope are all we have, and we make good use of both. How many will be around to partake of cold hash tomorrow night, and most important of all, who will they be? As usual, there are no answers.

A wartime cartoon comes to mind as it pictures a group of raggedy-assed miserable-looking infantrymen trudging through the rain and mud. The caption states simply: "Fresh troops moving up to the front," with today's little trek providing a perfect example. The hard truth is that most battles are fought by hungry, thirsty men on the verge of exhaustion. They manage, somehow, to put aside that basic concern for personal safety, live in the most abysmal discomfort, and then push themselves beyond the point of reason. Even more amazing is the fact that, with all this, they still hold on to at least a semblance of a sense of humor. The damned thing may, on occasion, be somewhat hard to find but is seldom lost for long.

Morning comes, perhaps too soon this day, as we stir our tired bones and grab another few bites of cold rations. A cup of warm coffee helps and will no doubt be the high point of the day. Then, with breakfast over, weapons are given a final check, ammo belts filled, and our supply of hand grenades replenished. Finally, safeties are pushed to the *off* position, and we are ordered to fix bayonets. Not the sort of moves that suggest even the remotest possibility of a good day.

The plan is for us to pass through the Marines occupying the front lines and then advance until contact is made with other Marine units on our right and somewhat ahead of us. Sounds easy, but the Japanese are holding a sort of knob in front of the lines and just happen to be dug in directly on the course we have been ordered to take. Artillery and mortar support will not be available as the fighting will take place too close to our lines. So, the dirty job will have to be done the hard way, with rifles and, as a last resort, bayonets.

Just a couple of squads holed up out there, we are told; knock them out as you go by. In reality, it is more like a force of two hundred, and they are equipped with a goodly number of machine guns in addition to an ample supply of hand grenades. To enhance their position and make life more difficult for us, the enemy has cut narrow "fire trails" through the jungle. Like small tunnels, they are only a few inches wide and are cut just above the ground, allowing the Japs to see us as we move toward them but hidden in such a way that we have little chance of spotting the small openings. Then, as a "morale booster," it is again impressed upon us that in the event of being hit, fall to the side if at all possible. Falling forward is to be riddled all the way to the ground.

Although one might be hard pressed to find much real enthusiasm for today's task, there is nevertheless a feeling that this is a job that has to be done, and there is not the slightest doubt about our ability to do it. However, with final instructions from platoon and squad leaders, apprehension and, along with it, a suspicion that fear will not be far behind. The order to move out is given quietly and we begin one more journey into hell. "Please God, see me through this day. Don't let me suffer too long."

Finally, as we make our way uphill and pass through the unit on the front lines, they wish us luck, thankful that someone else has the "glory" today. Just one tired, miserable group of Marines moving past more of the same, and there are no smiles in either group. The small battle to be fought here in this stinking jungle will not make the newspapers, but some of us and some of our enemy will die, and we wonder if anyone will really give a damn. That is surely one of the little horrors of this jungle war: that no one knows, and no one cares.

Crossing the ridgeline, we move downhill with my platoon attacking on the extreme right. The going is fairly good at this point as the Japanese have yet to see us and the slope is not too steep, although we are hampered, as usual, by the ever-present jungle. Then, with an awful suddenness, the good times are over as we are discovered by enemy machine guns. A few are hit in the first burst of fire; the rest continue as fear quickly begins to tear at our insides. We would like to lay on the ground, would like to get away from the terror, but we cannot.

As our attack carries us deeper into this thing, we come across dead Marines and note that some were undoubtedly killed while trying to recover bodies of those lost in previous attempts on this position. In this hellish existence, it is imperative that we care for our wounded and see that our dead are not left to rot on the battlefield. Sometimes we fail, but not for lack of trying. Continuing our advance, machine-gun fire increases as the enemy becomes certain of our intentions, and now, adding to the hell, mortar shells explode along the hillside. Danger is all around, and it is scary as hell, yet we cannot see a damn thing to shoot at. Then, as if enemy fire is not enough, a buddy is killed by his own hand grenade. Carrying it in his back pocket, the pin somehow came out and the damned thing exploded before he could get rid of it. I can just imagine his panic, knowing that he had only a few seconds to save himself. "War is hell," must be the understatement of all time.

The gentle slope down into a ravine is getting steeper, and our advance begins to slow under the steady enemy fire. Along with this, visibility is now limited to a few yards, or, in some cases, a few feet, giving most of us the uneasy feeling of being alone in this hellish place. Fear seems to dominate everything, and never knowing what that next step will bring is a special kind of terror.

Suddenly, the man on my right sags to the ground. Thinking he has either been hit or has seen some sign of the enemy, I drop down and call softly: "What's up, are you okay?" No answer but it sounds like he is crying. I screw up my courage and crawl over beside him. "What's wrong, are you hurt?" He won't, or perhaps can't, answer and continues sobbing. I can find no sign of a wound and figure he just got to that point where he could take no more. I hadn't really thought about it before, but now I find that it is no easy thing watching a buddy go to pieces. My own fear keeps me from thinking straight, but I finally decide to take off his gear and try to get him moving back up the hill. He isn't able to help, so I take my knife and cut away his pack and cartridge belt. He still won't budge, his mind somewhere else, away from all this horror. In desperation, I yell at him, commanding him to move. "Get your Goddamn ass up that hill." He moves a few feet, proving that old habits are hard to break. Whenever he stops, I yell some more, curse him, and, in so doing, scare the hell out of myself. Finally, he is out of sight, and I move carefully downhill to resume my position with the squad. The Japanese are still seventy-five to a hundred yards up ahead, but our advance seems to have come to a halt, and the report is that some units are pinned down. We haven't seen any of the bastards yet, but they sure as hell know where we are.

After a short delay, my platoon is ordered to break off and move down a canyon on our right flank, then attack from the rear. This turns out to be another of those easier-said-than-done jobs as the canyon is steep and heavily overgrown with jungle. As ordered, however, we spend a couple of exhausting hours hacking away at the miserable stuff and finally get in position to renew the attack. Naturally, we face another steep hill. Only this time, we have to fight our way up the damned thing. In addition, we are soon found out and come under fire again, thus confirming the day's original lousy expectations. Along with the sharp crackle of machine-gun fire coming from the crest of the hill, snipers try to pick us off from the treetops, and adding to the misery, these snipers are well-supplied with hand grenades. Move up a few yards or a few feet, then hit the ground. Wait a few minutes then, if still alive, do it again. That's general idea and what we have been ordered to do. Fear never leaves as bullets clip the bushes around us and grenades explode in our midst. The ground has become our best friend, and it is so hard to leave this friend and dash forward. Being on the attack, we must move and give them many targets while they remain hidden and rarely seen.

This seeming unfairness is, however, just one part of the hell. There are many others, and I manage to find one as I struggle forward. As usual, the Japs open up, and in diving for the ground, I get caught on something or another and wind up suspended in midair. Wondering all the while if this is it, I work frantically to get free and pray for help. It really is panic time as bullets zip around and, although the whole thing probably takes only a matter of seconds, the agony seemed like it would never end. In this place, small things are important, and it is such a relief to get back with my old friend, the ground. "Thanks, God." My grenade bag, the one the nice ladies in New Zealand knitted for me, caught a branch. That is the end of the bag—I tear it off, stuff a couple of grenades in my pockets, and leave the damned thing to rot on the hillside.

Suddenly, a new and—for us at least—welcome sound is heard. Up until now, the only machine-gun fire on this side of the hill has been Japanese. However, this sad state of affairs is finally over as one of our gun crews gets in position to lend a hand. The main difficulty being, although we call this place a hill, on this side it's more like a damned cliff. The gun crew opens up with an unusually long burst just to let us know that help has arrived, and it is music to our ears. "Take that, you miserable bastards!" It's almost like a movie with the cavalry coming to the rescue, and our morale goes up a notch. Unfortunately, however, this small taste of euphoria does not last, and it is soon back to fear.

The day has been long and bitter, a real son of a bitch, but we have finally eliminated most of the snipers and have no doubt killed many of the Japanese dug in up ahead. However, there is still plenty of fire coming from the hilltop, and that fire, along with the steepness of the slope and the damn jungle, keeps our progress to a slow crawl. Finally, having been at this all day (damn if we didn't miss lunch again), frustration sets in as we get within yards of our objective, and there are vague thoughts of rushing the Japs and getting the damn misery over with. The other side to this is, of course, that we could well get our asses killed and, deep down, there is still some small reluctance to giving up, too easily at least, even our miserable lives. And, besides, the thought of cold steel is never a particularly pleasant one. Fortunately, those who give the orders are not burdened by such petty considerations.

However, these thoughts are soon overshadowed by a different, if not less serious, problem: daylight. It is beginning to fade, and in the jungle, when it goes, it goes fast—leaving us with some nasty choices. To consider abandoning the attack, after gaining so much bitter ground, goes against the grain, but the obvious difficulty in holding our position on this steep slope after dark finally dictates the hard decision, and we are ordered to withdraw to the bottom of the hill, to resume our attack in the morning.

With mixed feelings then, we again break off contact and slowly make our way down. On one hand, there is the miserable thought that this damned hill will have to be fought for all over again. On the other, we perhaps have another night to live, and we are bushed. We reach somewhat level ground as it turns dark and are ordered to dig in for the night. Instead, we just fall down in a state of complete exhaustion, and no one gives a good Goddamn. The rigors of the last two days, piled on top of the last month, have literally wiped us out. More dead than alive, most would consider it a blessing just to be taken out of our misery.

Waking at first light, we look around and laugh at ourselves, proving that our sense of humor is still alive. Men, or things that somewhat resemble men, lay strewn about where they fell. A scroungier, more disheveled bunch would be hard to find. Again, I marvel that dirty, stinking, ordinary men can find the will to live out this horrible existence day after miserable day. Yet, most seem to find an inner strength that allows them to keep going even when certain that the future holds only more of the same.

Then, as we get our gear on, reload weapons, and prepare to renew the attack, a minor miracle occurs. An early patrol, sent out to reconnoiter, has returned with word that the Japs have done the unbelievable and pulled back during the night. Skeptical at first, this sort of thing being almost unheard of, we are soon assured that it is all true. What luck; we could have jumped for joy except that we have forgotten how. We do accept this bit of good fortune, however certain that it will not last.

The fight for this particular hill was just one part of a larger battle for control of a river junction known as the Piva Forks. Thousands of men fought bitterly to see who would have this miserable piece of ground, and although the Japanese have been pushed a little deeper into this stinking jungle, there is no time to savor our small victory as we are immediately ordered to push on, to continue the attack.

The days slip by but not easily as we constantly battle the enemy or the elements and quite often both. As casualties and disease take their toll, our numbers dwindle, and it is a rare day that we are not sick with something. Many have malaria and keep going only because of our daily ration of Atabrine, the tablet tossed into our mouths to be certain we take it. Forever alternating between dysentery and constipation, we are also plagued with large festering sores called tropical ulcers as well as various forms of fungus and jungle rot. Our feet are an absolute mess, and we have terrible rashes between our legs, due to our skivvies (underwear) having long since rotted away. In addition, lack of sleep along with physical and mental exhaustion is literally tearing us apart. Still, there is no end in sight. By now, the only reality in this insane world is us, and we are no longer even certain about us. Hardly knowing one another a year ago, we have become closer than brothers as we now live and die only for each other and, in some inexplicable way, the Marine Corps. The world is just the little spot we occupy today as we hear nothing of what goes on elsewhere. "This too shall pass," but when, God?

As you might imagine, then, our miseries take many forms, with some more or less expected while others seem to appear at inopportune times. In the latter category, I have been battling dysentery on and off for some time and, on this particular night, the unpleasant feeling has become especially worrisome with an hour or so still before dawn. Unable to leave my foxhole, of course, and not relishing a pants-cleaning chore, I find myself in rather extreme misery as I try to fight this distressing urge, the helmet bit not really an option because we made our foxhole too small. Then, just as I am about to lose the battle, daylight appears and I bolt out of our little home, scrape out a shallow hole a few feet away, and with an almost exquisite sense of relief, let nature do its thing. Although of little consequence compared to our more extreme suffering, this incident perhaps makes the small point that even minor discomforts can at times be almost unbearable. I might add that I do not reach for the toilet paper because we do not have any and have not had any since the first days of the campaign. This, then, is yet another of the small but annoying miseries as we are forced to use leaves, hoping they are not the poisonous kind, or whatever else is handy. Letters from home are never thrown away.

This is probably as good a time as any for a brief look at our resupply abilities and priorities. To begin with, we do not have any supplies except those which we go back and get ourselves, this little chore usually being added to an already miserable day's advance. These little treks are sometimes just a matter of a few hundred weary yards while, on others, the distance and the loads are backbreaking. As far as priorities go, it is all very simple: ammunition is first; water is next; food, if there is room, comes after that. There is no other category, so we are spared the hassle of trying to decide what else to bring.

A couple of weeks into December, we find ourselves on part of a mountain chain called "Hill 1000." To make it tougher for the Japs to infiltrate, it is explained, we are ordered to dig in on the forward slope, up near the ridge. We think this a poor choice, being so exposed, but as usual, do what we must and make our foxholes as secure as possible. Soon after, word comes down that the advance is over, that we are going to build a defensive line at this point and let the Japs have the rest of the miserable place. Building defenses is not really our cup of tea, but hopefully, this is a sign that our stay on this hellhole is nearing an end. As expected, the chore turns out to be much hard work as we are ordered to dig deeper foxholes, install overhead cover, and string barbed wire entanglements in front of the lines. In addition, daily work parties are sent back for ammo, rations, and other necessities. This is particularly difficult as the trail up here is steep, narrow, and slippery. It goes without saying that we also take our regular turn on patrol—there being no rest, only hell, for the stinking foot sloggers.

My platoon members carrying supplies up to Hill 1000. I'm carrying the box in the front.

Difficult as it may be to imagine anything disrupting this idyllic existence, a lousy sniper is doing his best to do just that. The son of a bitch is hidden in a stand of tall trees overlooking the mountain's only water supply, and so far at least, no one has been able to spot the bastard. The water is just a tiny trickle and is situated in a hard-to-reach but very exposed location, so as one might expect, there is no big demand for the water detail. The Marine Corps, however, handles these things very simply. When your name is called, it is considered that you have volunteered, no matter what the chore. We have, of course, had to contend with snipers on numerous other occasions, but this miserable SOB is beginning to be a damn nuisance.

Fortunately, he seems to be a lousy shot but still manages to turn an otherwise mundane chore into something of an adventure. However, with more important things to occupy our time, we more or less put up with the inconvenience for a day or two, then someone finally kills the bastard, and filling a canteen goes back to being a somewhat ordinary affair.

Even though we work like hell to build up our lines, the Japs are still out there, still determined to kill as many of us as they can. One way is with artillery, and it isn't long before we find out just how vulnerable these positions are. Of the many and varied miseries we face, artillery fire is probably the most devastating. The explosions literally shake the earth, the noise is almost unbearable, and never knowing where the next one will hit is a terror that can only be known by those who have had the misfortune of being in the way of the damned things. Fear ties our stomachs in knots while we hug the ground, praying that the shells somehow miss our foxhole. They must hit someplace, but not here, God, not here—please. Though we all pray, not all will be saved, and we constantly wonder if we really are part of a plan or if it, perhaps, is just luck of the draw.

On one such night, our section of the line is hit especially hard, and with our foxhole being one that escaped relatively undamaged, my buddy and I are ordered to separate in order to better cover our assigned area—attacks in strength often following heavy artillery fire. I am then ordered to a position where both men have been wounded, finding, as I crawl in, a distinct aroma of blood mixing with the already-dank smell of earth. This odor lingers due to the rather confined space (we have finally installed overhead cover of a sort), and with it comes a feeling of discomfort. I don't know if it is the smell or that a little bit of hell had so recently struck this hole or whether it is just due to my having been moved from my old hole, which seemed rather safe because it didn't get hit this time, into one that has this aura of bad luck about it.

· · · · · · ·

In any event, people like us attach a good deal of importance to small things and especially to those which might, remotely or not, have a bearing on our survival. However, we sometimes carry this a fair way beyond what ordinary folks would consider normal, and as a small example of this sort of thinking, I have made the rather important discovery that not fastening my helmet strap is somehow luckier than having it fastened. Feeling fortunate to have found this out early on, I now buckle the damned thing only when absolutely necessary. Do not get the idea, however, that I am so foolish as to depend on just one such amulet. I have others—all equally important.

My new buddy is a mortarman, ordered up from his position somewhat back of the front line to help fill the gaps. Although often near the thing and occasionally in the thing, these men find that there is a not-so-subtle difference when on the line, especially at night.

The days slip by, and the hillside becomes littered with shell holes—trees, bushes, and our positions torn from shrapnel, and those who are left shake at the slightest sound. Methinks we have been here too long.

Rumors have been making the rounds for some time, but now they say it is for sure that the Army will relieve us next week. It doesn't seem possible, after these last miserable months, that we are really that close. Now all we have to do is try to stay in one piece for a few more days. Beautiful news, however, and someone remembers that it is the day before Christmas. Christmas. What I wouldn't give to be home. It seems so far away now, and I wonder, more and more, if I am ever to see it again.

Then, in keeping with our rather protracted run of rotten luck, comes another of those sudden, nasty turnabouts. It is the platoon sergeant telling us to get our gear on, that we have been ordered out on patrol! "Son of a bitch, we were just out on patrol!"

"Tell it to the chaplain," is the sergeant's reply. He then explains that the morning patrol set off a land mine (one of those damned "Bouncing Betties" that jumps up and explodes about chest high) just outside the lines with several men being seriously wounded. We apparently drew the short straw and have been ordered to take their place—damn those miserable odds. That old sinking feeling returns, and we sense our good luck slipping away. We put on cartridge belts and helmets, grab our rifles, and move out.

Taking leave of the front lines, we move carefully downhill, watching closely for trip wires or anything that looks out of place. Our first chore is to set an ambush, hoping to catch an enemy patrol moving about, perhaps trying to do the same to us. We set up several hundred yards out and wait. After an hour or so and no customers, we proceed with the primary part of our mission. As a result of aircraft reconnaissance, this patrol has been ordered to scout an area deep in enemy territory. There is a suspicion that the Japanese are building up for a major offensive, so we have the job of pinpointing the location, determining their strength, and then, of course, getting the information back. Instead of the usual five or six of us, this patrol has at least twenty, which leads to the feeling that someone is expecting trouble on this little outing. We take note that the odds of our staying in one piece have just changed. The extra twelve or so consist of a special squad from division HQ. One member of this squad is a Thompson-toting friend of mine from boot camp.

Moving in single file, we travel through dense jungle and swamp, ford several rivers, and are now beyond our normal patrol zone. The farther we go, the scarier it gets, and we strain our senses trying to look everywhere at once while at the same time listening for the slightest out-of-place sound. The point man has the worst of it, as he must also keep our compass course while living with the ever-present thought that, when something happens, it will no doubt happen to him first. This being such a delightful job, we all get a turn at it. The more the afternoon wears on, the more we get the uneasy feeling of walking into some dark, alien world unsure of what to expect, yet expecting the worst.

Now, our quite regular late-afternoon rain begins, and it is a veritable downpour, adding more misery to an already miserable day. In addition, we should be thinking about heading back, but instead, we begin to see trails and other signs of enemy activity and so are ordered to continue. We do this with extreme caution, trying to see without being seen. However, as we pass more and more of these trails, the inescapable conclusion is that there are a lot of Japs around here and the report of a large buildup apparently is all too true. Along with this comes a growing awareness that we are completely on our own, that no cavalry will come should we run into trouble.

Much of the fighting was done in heavy rain and mud.

Although sure that our enemy is close by, we have seen none; yet, then, "son of a bitch, there's one over there." Sure enough, in a small clearing to our left, a lone sentry is sitting down, trying to heat his dinner in the pouring rain. The poor bastard looks almost as miserable as we feel. There is a short debate about killing him, but it is finally decided to let him be, at least for now. Leaving the Jap to his troubles, we push on, and the patrol leader decides some of us should scout a few of the trails. I get "lucky" and am ordered to check a faint path angling off to the right. After a few steps, I lose sight of the others and am immediately gripped by deep fear.

Fear has been with us all afternoon, but this is different, and I find that being alone in the jungle in the midst of the enemy is a special kind of terror. Without a doubt, misery does love company. Now rather thankful for the rain, I move as quietly as possible and worry over each step. The foliage is extremely dense along the path, providing much cover for those who would do me in, and even though wishing to hell that I was somewhere else, I manage to cover the distance as ordered. I see no Japs on this little stroll but am nevertheless struck with the uncomfortable feeling they are close by. Turning back, I am hit with an almost overpowering urge to take off running, and it takes all my willpower just to keep at a somewhat normal pace, the miserable expectation of a knife in the back dogging each step. The patrol is a welcome sight, and I allow my back muscles to relax just a bit.

With the many signs of recent activity, we wonder about not seeing more of the enemy and finally decide the downpour must be keeping them in their foxholes. Perhaps the rain is a blessing, even though we are soaked to the skin. We continue to move cautiously, most of us hoping we can see what we came to see and then get the hell out. It wasn't to be as, all of a sudden, *Bang-Bang*, *Rat-a-tat-tat* comes from up ahead. "Dirty son of a bitch, we're in for it now!" We immediately hit the deck as firing erupts all over the damn place. As I go down, my foot gets stuck between a couple of big roots, and I wind up laying over another one with my rear end sticking high in the air. Then, before I can free myself, an arm rises out of some nearby bushes, and a grenade comes sailing my way. "Holy Christ, I'm gonna get it for sure! Help me, God!"

The grenade lands about ten feet away while I quickly try to cram as much of me as possible into my helmet and wonder how bad it will be. Fully expecting the worst, the damn thing explodes and nothing, not even a scratch. "Thanks, God." Hardly able to believe my good luck, I waste no time getting untangled then take cover in those same roots. As I am scrambling around, a fellow with a pistol takes a shot at me from about ten yards away. My friend with the Thompson takes care of him with a couple of quick bursts. It takes no prompting for us to realize how serious our situation is, although we take some comfort in the fact that the Japanese are probably at least as confused as we are. Furthermore, if the bastards knew our relatively small number, we probably wouldn't last long—maybe we won't last long anyway.

We have apparently stumbled onto a hell of a lot more Japs than we expected. From the look of things, they are at least battalion strength, no doubt preparing to hit our lines, and they are damn sure not going to let us get back if they can help it. And now, added to the fact that we are outnumbered to beat hell, it is late in the day and we are a long way from "home," meaning it will be dark soon and our merely difficult situation will then be a desperate one. So, it isn't really hard to figure out that the longer we stay in this exposed position, the more chance the Japs have of getting organized and wiping us out. However, there have been no orders to fall back—or to do anything else, for that matter. In this miserable jungle war, we are quite often left to struggle on our own and, for better or for worse, we really have no choice but to hold to the bitter end—no matter what that may be.

Meanwhile, grenades pop along with automatic weapon and rifle fire as both sides try to find targets, though the thick brush and heavy rain allow few clear shots. This lack of visibility, though somewhat to our advantage, is nevertheless frustrating, and as a matter of fact, I feel damn lonely when I look around and see only the two men on either side of me, and it is not much help that they are some five yards away, barely visible in all this greenery. It is even more discouraging when we realize just what a downright mean and dangerous situation we are in, and for the first time, I begin to feel that this might be the end of it, that I may well be killed here in this stinking, Godforsaken piece of jungle.

Surrender, by the way, is really not an option for us. To begin with, the Corps does not look kindly on giving up for any reason. Added to that is the terrible reputation the Japs have when it comes to prisoner treatment—rumors of bayonet practice during the Guadalcanal Campaign still fresh in our minds. It may be understood then that some of us have vague thoughts of saving a last cartridge. Suddenly, the man on my left informs me that our patrol has become separated, that the section with the patrol leader pulled back, and in all the confusion, some of us didn't get the word. That sinking feeling sinks even further. Then, he says we are to slowly break off contact and try to find our way back to the lines. Thank God, anything is better than staying here. I pass the word to the man on my right. One at a time, we stop firing and crawl back, hopefully away from Japanese positions. It's still raining hard, and we wonder if that is His way of helping. Getting together some twenty yards back, we find that there are eight or nine in our little group and, feeling lucky as hell to have gotten this far, decide to make a run for it and hope for the best. Time, though, is a very real problem, and there is none to spare. We move out in single file, taking a compass heading that should get us back, but thick jungle prevents us from actually seeing any landmarks. Running at a trot whenever possible, we pass through a number of enemy positions, fully expecting to be cut down at any second. The whole thing is unreal as hell, and we just cannot believe that our luck can continue. Rain, keep coming—the harder, the better.

"Dirty, no-good son of a bitch, just what we need, a Goddamn swamp!" No time to look for a way around, so we just plow into the stinking slime. Looking back, we can't figure why the Japs are not right on our tail.

Our luck—or is it luck?—seems incredible, and as we become more engulfed in the swamp and somewhat hidden, we dare think that maybe, just maybe, we might get out of this damn thing yet. Funny, but I never realized, until now, just how lovely a swamp can be. Rain and now swamp—maybe He is helping us. Finally clear of the swamp but still looking over our shoulders, we are occasionally forced to stop and climb trees to get our bearings. Now there is just one last river and then about half a mile to the lines. "God, don't let us down now." Feeling every bit like sitting ducks, we wade across, still expecting the Japs to open up at any time.

The rain has slowed somewhat as we move into the last stretch of jungle, and there is a sense of relief in getting this far, but daylight is fading fast. That brings us to other problems as we remember the rule which considers any movement after dark to be the enemy. It would be a hell of a note if our own troops fire on us but, hopefully, they have been alerted to the fact that we're still out. I sure hope so. Then, as we get close to the lines, land mines and booby traps offer yet another threat. What a stinking shame if, after all this, we manage to set one of those damned things off. It turns dark as we reach the bottom of the hill, but the front lines are now only a couple hundred feet above us. "Just a little more, God, just a little more." We call out the password and that we are a recon patrol which ran into a little trouble. There is a momentary silence as we look uneasily back over our shoulders and then these wonderful words: "Come on home, all is forgiven." We wait while a guide is sent down to get us through the mines, then it is up the hill and into the lovely front lines. Earlier in the day, I just couldn't conceive of a way out of our predicament and felt I wasn't going to survive, yet as we approach our lines, and the miracle of our escape and survival begins to sink in, a friend behind me puts his hand on my shoulder reminding me of the date as he whispers, "Hey Swanee, it's Christmas Eve!" What a feeling, it's Christmas Eve and we are back "home," back in our beautiful foxhole. Thanks, God.

The rest of the patrol, as we hoped, got back earlier and alerted the front lines to watch for us, then passed their information on the Japanese positions back to artillery. Fire was held up, giving us time to get in the clear; now however, the "Long Toms" open up with a hellish barrage. Laying in our foxholes, we listen to the outgoing shells with the satisfaction of knowing we accomplished that which we were sent out to do, yet at the same time, feeling just a bit sorry for the poor bastards out there. They are catching all kinds of hell. This time it's them; next time it will no doubt be us.

The rumors of relief are apparently true, and in a few days, it will all be over, at least for now. Even so, we are ever so careful, hoping against hope that our luck can hold, but the damned artillery and snipers—don't they know we're leaving soon, that we almost have it made? The last days go by slowly. I guess it wasn't meant to be easy.

Finally, after two long and miserable months, almost all spent on the front lines, relief arrives in the form of the US Army. A welcome sight, though they look so young and clean. I wonder if we looked that way a couple of months—or was it years?—ago. They take over our positions, and we sense that they look to us for assurance that it will not be too bad. However, based on our miserable experience, we have no such assurance to give. The Army officially takes over in late afternoon and we are turned loose, to be at the beach by morning for embarkation. Grabbing our rifles and gear, we sincerely wish the soldiers good luck and head back, away from "Hill 1000." It is a giddy feeling to be free, to have the shackles of fear lifted, if only for a while.

Our first priority is to locate a "Seabee" camp (construction battalion), hoping they will take pity and allow us to share a meal with them. We have heard they feed good, and it has also been rumored that, on occasion, they have taken in those who are less fortunate. After some searching, we do locate such a place and, although not expecting company, they act the gracious host and set an extra plate for us. We think that we must have accidentally been misdirected to Heaven.

In the morning, we thank our hosts, then, for the first time since our arrival, move out of the jungle and the darkness into a world that seems unconcerned with fear and misery and feel as strangers. The sense of suffering that has been so much a part of our lives is somehow missing as men go about various tasks, seemingly unaware that death and terror exist only a short distance away. Perhaps it has always been this way, or perhaps it is just that the jungle hides so well its unpleasantness.

Though recognizing little on our journey to the coast, we do pass one particular area that had been fought over in the first days of the campaign and find that it is now an airstrip and home to a long row of Pappy Boyington's Corsairs, as a matter of fact. it was here that the Seabees, in their usual eagerness to get the job done, cleared the jungle up to and then some distance beyond the front lines, this while we were out on patrol and unable to look after our interests. They, however, showed much class as they worked carefully around our "homes" and our "precious belongings," even going so far as to leave a nice clump of jungle around each foxhole. In reality, this was the same as putting up a sign indicating to the Japs where we were; however, it was a beautiful thought and that's what counts. As it turned out, we had a quiet night and then were ordered to move up in the morning, so it didn't matter all that much, although we did manage a chuckle over their kind gesture. Seeing the airfield, here in the midst of what once was a thick stand of jungle, brings home the point that, to a large degree, this is what our misery and suffering was all about—a place to park airplanes.

Before leaving, however, there is still one important task, and that is to visit at least some of the small cemeteries scattered about the jungle. This will become a sort of ritual as we search out the rows of white crosses, taking a moment to pay our respects to those whose luck ran out and to again wonder why them and not us and then to wonder which names will be on the next campaign's crosses.

At the beach, we leave as we came, though not quite so noisily, and then board the USS *President Hayes* for the return trip to good old Guadalcanal.

The campaign for Bougainville has been two months of unending hell; however, I chose to leave out the blood, the maggots, and the blowflies. The Japanese proved to be a brutally tough enemy who gave no quarter, nor did we. I wish that I could say that the fighting will get easier, but the reality is that it will not and, in fact, will only get worse. Though we often ask for a glimpse into the future, God, in his wisdom, sees that our wish is not granted.

My rather emaciated company on our way to the beach from Hill 1000 after the Army takeover of our positions.

GUADALCANAL AGAIN

*The infantryman will talk about them,
think about them, and dream about them.
He will long to be with them.*

January 1944

Finally back aboard ship (Taj Mahal, what in the Goddamned hell was I thinking of), those who "made it" make a hot shower their number one priority. God, what a feeling to get these rotted, stinking dungarees off and, for the first time in two months, feel clean. Though drenched almost daily and even occasionally fording rivers, these "baths" were of little help as we always seemed to find mud or swamp soon after. Now, feeling safe (the ultimate of luxuries) and clean once again, we look forward to some of the other creature comforts so sorely missed—namely, a decent meal, an uninterrupted night's sleep, an actual sit-down head and, in a way, the most luxurious of all, a drink of water whenever desired. You see, we do not ask for much, but to be honest, once these small wants are satisfied, we will find others—that being the peculiar nature of the beast.

Speaking as we are of luxuries, the heads aboard troop transports deserve some mention. These so-called "bathrooms" are, by necessity, fairly large rooms with the plumbing consisting solely of metal troughs installed wall to wall. These troughs then, in order to justify the term "sit down," have wooden slats placed across them at strategic intervals with water constantly flowing through several of these rooms until it exits into the ocean. As one might expect, then, answering nature's call can be rather interesting as the water and whatever is in it sloshes back and forth as well as up and over with the motion of the ship, this being even more of a hazard in rough weather. So, even though we have advanced to this lofty new position in life, one must be constantly alert while sitting; for in addition to the expected, it is not unknown for some wiseass in the adjacent head to set fire to a wad of paper and then allow and even encourage this flaming wad to float down the trough. The adventure seemingly never ends and, as I write, the term artful dodger somehow comes to mind.

Now, with the *Hayes* and other ships of our convoy again anchored off Guadalcanal, we climb down the nets and head for home, looking forward to sacking out in our comfortable old camp—but no such luck. In our absence, some other outfit moved in, and we have to build another one. Dirty bastards, they've done it to us again. Tired, sick, most with festering sores, we surely thought they would give us a bit of rest after these last bitter months. Instead, we hack away at the jungle, as before, cursing our luck and the damned war. With open sores making walking painful and hard work a misery, the Navy doctors want to put us on light duty until these tropical ulcers get somewhat better. However, the Marine Corps is against what they consider a blatant attempt at mollycoddling and, as you might expect, the doctors lose and so do we. We, of course, do what has to be done, but not without our usual and considerable griping and cursing.

We soon discover that the old Guadalcanal is no more and, in fact, has changed considerably during our absence. Our old friend, "Washing Machine Charlie," is gone—a victim of the new airstrips on Bougainville—and the island now has a large PX (post exchange), although the damn lines are a million miles long, give or take a few. This semblance of civilization is probably due to the island having become one of our main forward bases in the South Pacific and, as a result of that status, is now home to a number of Marine and Army units in addition to ours. Supplying this large group of men and getting them ready for upcoming campaigns has no doubt put a strain on available manpower. Still, it is somewhat of a surprise to see bushy-haired natives marching alongside Marine working parties. Though they look out of place, they are eager to help and seem to really enjoy being part of all this excitement.

However, we are probably witness to the last hurrah for Guadalcanal, as changes are in the wind that will turn the place into just another piece of backwater. The reality is that the war is passing this place by, and June will find us in the Central Pacific preparing to hit the Marianas.

We, not being privy to these plans and hampered by the rather limited view from our foxhole, see only more jungle and more swamp in an endless progression of landings on places like Truk, Rabaul, New Ireland, and God only knows what others. If they are all to be as long and miserable as Bougainville, it is going to be a son of a bitch of a war.

They still toss an Atabrine tablet in my mouth each day, usually in chow line, but the effect seems to be wearing off as I manage to come down with occasional attacks of malaria. Though most of us suffer from these attacks or have other ailments, few turn in to the hospital, and I am not altogether sure why. However, aches and pains notwithstanding, the damned camp is eventually finished, our sores begin to heal, and with replacements newly arrived from the States, we get on to serious preparations for the next campaign.

As the new men come in, we who are now old-timers and combat veterans watch and are somewhat taken aback by their eagerness to get into action. Is it possible that we felt that way only a few months ago? Seeing combat up close has, I fear, taken the bloom off the rose, and we now know that its main ingredients are only misery, fear, and death. Still, for those who have yet to experience the hell, there is the illusion of excitement and adventure.

The middle of March sees us, once again, packing seabags for storage, squaring away combat gear, and boarding ship. The plan calls for us to hit a place called New Ireland. Then, after climbing up the nets and settling in and while preparations are being made to get under way, we receive unexpected news. The invasion bas been called off due to a belief that the island can be bypassed as well as an expectation of heavy casualties. New men are disappointed by this unusual turn of events, the old-timers are secretly relieved. The Marine Corps, not being one to waste, orders a practice landing, which we carry out. Then it is back to camp and to training for the next landing, wherever in hell that might be.

Shortly after our return, a rather notable event takes place on Guadalcanal as the Ninth Marine Regiment parades in pressed khaki. A small thing, perhaps, but how in the hell do uniforms get pressed out here in the boondocks? The answer is that they are neatly folded, then placed between the mattress pads and canvas of our cots, and slept on for a few nights. Where there is a will, there is usually a way, and the Corps, a taskmaster in the use of "incentives," expects that you will find it. This parade is supposedly to build morale, but we suspect it is mostly for the officers' benefit and are not particularly eager about marching around in this tropical heat; but then, who in hell are we? Which reminds me of our company song, and the damn thing goes something like this: "Hidey-didey, Christ almighty, who in the hell are we? Zim-Zam, Goddamn, we're (C) Company. Oh, we're dilly sons of bitches and we'd rather—" Well, you get the idea. The dirty little ditty goes on and on with each group singing pretty much the same song, changing only the (letter) to correspond with its own identity. And it is not especially suited to mixed company.

During this in-between-campaigns time, I am surprised by a couple of unexpected visitors. Relaxing with a cigar on a Sunday afternoon, I look up to find one of my boyhood pals strolling into the tent. He is also a Gyrene (a Marine) but in a different division, and we manage to get together two or three times before the war forces us to move on. Chatting about home and the old days is a real treat, and as he is a recent arrival from the States, his visit makes that other world seem just a little closer. However, it isn't long before events begin catching up with us, and as our regiments make final preparations to move out, we find time to wish each other luck—unaware that we are both to hit the same place: Guam. Unfortunately, his luck takes a turn for the worse and he is seriously wounded in the bitter fighting. In fact, his poor mother received a telegram notifying her that he'd been killed in action and did not learn he had survived for some time.

My other visitor is a cousin whom I had met briefly some years ago, and although he and I are in the same division, we serve in different regiments. He also went through the miseries of Bougainville but seems to feel, more so than most, that those Goddamned odds are catching up with us. He has somehow lost that tiny spark of hope and sees little chance of our getting out of this thing in one piece. Though most of us get these feelings from time to time—they seem to go hand in hand with this line of work—he is so discouraged that I begin to wonder if he has had some premonition or if he perhaps senses something that eludes the rest of us. Do we, or at least, do some of us, receive a signal of sorts before it ends? It is important for us to know such things as we live each day with the certainty that many of us are not going to make it, and we constantly wonder if there really is some forewarning. Then, toward the end of May, the winds are once again telling us that time is running out, so we say goodbye and wish each other luck, wondering always if we are to meet again.

Some months later, I learn that my cousin was killed in the fight for Guam, and I think back to that time on Guadalcanal, wondering all the more if he had somehow been given a glimpse into the future. And along with news of his death, comes word that my cousin, Corporal Arthur "Pud" Anderson, has been awarded the Navy Cross for his part in the bitter fight to retake Guam.

It is so hard when it is a friend, and I begin to wonder, with this thing looking like it could go on forever, if any of us are to be spared or if it will just be a matter of going on until our luck finally runs out.

GUAM

*The thing works because the man next
to you is certain that you will be there,
and you know damn well he will be there.*

June 2, 1944

Once again, seabags are packed for storage and we are off on another one, marching to the beach with full packs and combat gear. As usual, we wade out to our familiar old Higgins boat and prepare to board ship. For this trip, we draw the USS *President Hayes*, by now an old friend, as she brought us back from Bougainville in addition to hosting us for a week of practice landings off New Zealand. On our last such departure, we were issued ammo and combat rations after boarding ship. This time, however, they (and you know who the hell they are) have chosen to load us down before leaving camp, and we have one hell of a time climbing up the damn nets. Going down the ratty old things with a hundred pounds on our backs is one thing, climbing up is quite another.

We leave Guadalcanal for good this time, and we leave with somewhat mixed feelings. A hellhole, some would say, but it was "home," and we wonder now what new kind of hellhole awaits. Then, as we get underway, word is passed down that our division is going to hit the island of Guam, landing on a beach near Asan Point. They tell us it is doubtful that the Japanese will look kindly on our visit and to expect heavy casualties. Somewhat smaller than Bougainville, Guam has less jungle but many more caves and pillboxes, with artillery and mortar fire expected to be heavy. We are duly impressed. There is one good thing, though, and that is we land in reserve instead of the first wave, as before. We get another break, of sorts, being temporarily assigned to company headquarters for the first part of this campaign. I accept this little gift of luck but, again, do not plan on it lasting.

Although our heading is north for this operation, the convoy makes a slight detour to the east as we stop at Kwajalein, in the Marshall Islands, for staging. Then, after a few days and the addition of more ships, the convoy reforms and heads for the invasion of Saipan, where we are in floating reserve. The battle of Saipan turns out to be so tough that the Guam operation has to be postponed. There are not enough ships to support both landings, and to make it worse, the Japanese fleet arrives for an all-out battle to save the Marianas. Our convoy, then, with its many troop transports, is forced to change direction and heads back to the Marshall Islands, this time anchoring at Eniwetok Atoll.

We remain in this rather protected area for several weeks, getting off the ship only for occasional practice landings and maneuvers. All in all, we spend seven weeks aboard ship on this voyage, and cooped up as we are, that is a hell of a long time. The things are uncomfortable at best and, as you might expect, are seldom at their best, with the heat and humidity being damn near unbearable, the troop compartments crowded and reeking of sweat. However, the real hell of it is that after a few hours or perhaps minutes on Guam, we will be rather envious of those remaining on board.

Speaking of discomfort, and you can be Goddamned sure that we do almost constantly, I touched briefly on the subject of flies a bit earlier with the particular problem then being an annoying habit of crawling in the damned ointment at inopportune times. That is revolting enough; however, it is not the worst of it as we quickly discover during our occasional junkets to the small islands making up this atoll. With the battle for these islands having taken place just a few months ago, part of the residue from that fighting is an unbelievable horde of starving, angry flies. How the devilish things arrive on these isolated pieces of coral, I do not know, but nature, in its unfathomable way, sees that they do. The problem being that, after completing their assigned work, they are then stuck on these places for whatever period of time they can survive unless, of course, providence should intervene. We then, once again being in the right place at the right time, have seemingly become, at least in the flies' view, the instrument of divine intervention.

We land and the bastards are all over us as we try to eat the baloney sandwiches that the Navy always provides for lunch, and it is a race to get the food to our mouths before it turns black. Finally, then, as we board our Higgins boats for a return to the ship, the miserable devils, somehow sensing that it is now or never, literally cover the boat and our helmets like a coat of black paint. Fortunately, the pesky things are blown off by ocean breezes before we reach the ship, but the misery is the same each time we go ashore.

Life at sea does have its good side, though, as we get a break from incessant training, and chow is generally better than in camp. Although troopship mess is ordinary by even the most liberal interpretation of the word, it surpasses camp food by a considerable margin. Dessert is even routinely served at dinner, the cook's favorite being bread pudding, so I guess that is our favorite too, although a complaint is heard now and then about raisins that move. Breakfast is typically Navy, being various and sundry items on a shingle (toast) alternating with dehydrated eggs and, on red-letter days, pancakes. The real treat, though, is an apple or an orange every morning, items we rarely see in the field.

Eventually, the Japanese fleet is defeated, Saipan more or less secured, and with that, our unexpected vacation ends. Now, with these not inconsiderable details out of the way, the convoy prepares for sea and once again heads west, this time for our long-delayed landing on Guam.

July 21, 1944

"D-Day" again, and I wonder how many are still to go. This one is somewhat different as we land in a later wave and will be able to watch some of the show instead of being the show. The landing routine having by now become quite familiar, at least to us old-timers, we listen as the loudspeaker issues the usual stream of instructions and the crew goes about its business of readying the ship to land troops.

There is, however, a noticeable difference in the size of this show. At Bougainville, naval support consisted mainly of a few destroyers, with troop transports firing their deck guns for good measure. This time, there are battleships and cruisers all over the place, with carriers even visible on the horizon. The bombardment is heavy as shells chip away at cliffs to our left and explosions cover the beach. Hard to believe the enemy can live through this terror, but we know all too well that he does. Now, a layer of smoke and dust begins to form over the island and, once again, we wonder what horrors lie waiting. The new men are eager to get in and see what it is all about, the old-timers already know it is only hell that we will find.

There is a temporary halt in the bombardment as a squadron of Marine Corsairs roars in strafing the beach, flying so low that they almost touch the few palm trees left standing. They make several passes, flying dangerously close to the ground, doing everything possible to help their fellow Marines about to hit this unfriendly beach. Finally, the Corsairs complete their work and move inland as the first waves, in their amphibious tractors, slowly head for shore. At this point, a group of ships similar to small destroyers begins to move along the coast. They are new rocket-firing ships and will lay down a curtain of fire just before the first wave arrives. Suddenly, the ships let go their load of rockets, firing one rack after another. In a matter of minutes, thousands of these things explode on the beach, and we almost feel sorry for the Japs. The first wave, however, has no time for such foolishness as, at this moment, they are looking directly at hell. Seconds later, the am-tracs climb up on the beach, the Marines jump out, and the battle is on.

My company, due to land about an hour after the first wave, gets the signal, and we climb down the nets into our waiting amphibious tractors. Then, after forming up with other am-tracs in our wave, we head for the beach and another little journey into the unknown. I know a little of what to expect and yet I don't know. Each landing, each miserable day is different. The tractor churns slowly through the water and it appears that the fighting has moved into low-lying hills a few hundred yards or so from the beach; however, enemy shells continue to fall along the shoreline, sending up plumes of spray when they explode in the water. In reserve or not, this place looks dangerous.

Then, some four hundred yards from shore, our tractor hits the coral reef and is forced to climb at a hellishly steep angle to get over the edge. Now, after thinking that the open ocean was choppy and rough, we find it is something else here on the reef. We go straight up then straight down, at the same time leaning at almost impossible angles, seemingly about to tip over time after time. Talk about the frying pan and the fire. We grab for anything handy, hanging on for dear life.

It looks bad as we approach the beach, shell holes everywhere, trees shattered and uprooted, damaged amtracs and equipment scattered about. No one is walking; they are either running or hugging the ground. Our tractor climbs up on the sand, stops suddenly, and we immediately jump over the side, hitting the ground hard. It's a good six-foot drop, and with our heavy gear, we feel all of it. The beach has apparently been cleared of enemy, but there is still a fair amount of confusion due mainly to the continuing artillery and mortar fire. This fire being mean and downright miserable, we waste a bit of valuable time getting organized, then move inland as shells explode in and around us. Putting it mildly, it is scary as hell!

A large rice paddy lies between the beach and the hills ahead and, in crossing, we are saddened to find many dead Marines in our path. Victims of the fighting a short while ago, they lie as they fell. It has been a terrible morning for some, and the day is far from over. We move past the torn bodies of our buddies, hoping and praying that we will be spared, yet knowing in our hearts that many will not. Fear is on me again, fear of death of course, but I have found that it is relatively easy to resign oneself to death and, on occasion, even welcome the thing. It is really the violence, the pain, the suddenness, and unpredictability of events that tear our insides. We cannot be sure of anything, not the next step or the next second, and that is the real terror. As we arrive at the base of these low hills, I am ordered to go with the jeep driver to find ammo and water. The driver and I pile into the jeep and head down a narrow road crossing the rice paddy. Jap artillery apparently thinks we are a good target as shells hit just behind us then just in front. Uh-oh! The driver slams on the brakes; we jump out and hit the deck as a shell explodes near where we would have been. Back in the jeep, we continue down the road but are forced to repeat this scene a time or two before reaching our supplies. My luck is holding but it is still scary as hell. Nothing is easy on this kind of a day, but we finally locate a supply dump, pick up our stuff, and head back, repeating the process. Can't believe we made it to the beach and near dark now, and we are ordered to dig in. Though vital to our survival, it is just another of our many miseries that we have to dig a Goddamn hole in the ground every night. Reserve is over as my company takes its place on the line and prepares to attack in the morning. We do not have to wait until morning for the terror, however, as artillery and mortar shells explode through the night. Some land close enough to scatter me with dirt; one explodes on the edge of my foxhole. I pray to God and wish to hell that I had dug in deeper.

Dawn comes and we have our usual stew or hash for breakfast, then we push on. In my temporary assignment, I miss much of the dog-eat-dog infantry fighting but am seldom far from the front and occasionally get caught up in the battles. Artillery and mortars don't seem to give a damn where I am or what I am doing. Strangely though, I miss that rather special feeling those in the line have for each other.

This feeling is no doubt born out of a sharing of misery and fear and is not likely to be understood outside this particular group.

The battle for Guam turns out to be tough and bloody, but I am not sure which kind of fighting is the hardest. Bougainville, with its stinking jungle and swamp, was long, miserable, and filled with almost constant terror; while this campaign, though destined to be shorter, seems more violent. It is all so damned hard, and it is no help that the old torments have followed us here. Never enough water is still a misery (in the tropics of all places) as we sweat like stuck pigs. When possible, we start out with two full canteens and try to avoid taking that first drink until noon. If we give in to our thirst too soon, the craving becomes so intense that the day's supply is gone in a couple of hours. When that happens, the rest of the day is pure agony as there is usually no more to be had. Then, on those days when we have little or none to start with, it is torture, pure and simple. Exhaustion catches up with us again as we go with little sleep, still in our two-man foxholes, always moving up. In this business, there are no eight-hour days, no weekends off, and certainly no evenings to relax. The days are a full twenty-four hours, and they come one right after the other.

This is a busy time for BARs and flamethrowers, as the enemy is holed up in caves, pillboxes, whatever he can find. It is the meanest kind of fighting and, even though the bastards are eventually done in, we pay dearly for our small victories. We imagine the Jap must be terrified in his last moments, yet the son of a bitch holds out to the bitter end. One minute we grudgingly admire his courage then, in the next, hate his miserable guts.

Forced to live day after day with this hate and our misery, we soon lose any pretense of compassion. The enemy, from our foxhole view, seems downright cruel and ruthless—no better than animals, and we respond in kind. By now, we have become completely indifferent to the sight of their mutilated bodies, though it hurts down deep to see ours, and it is a sad fact that the stench of decaying flesh follows wherever we go. It is also a fact that along with this hellish and unbelievably penetrating odor comes a variety of nature's tittle helpers. Maggots, in particular, are rather a marvel, and we often find ourselves watching as they go about their busy work. Blowflies, however, are something else. Even though engaged in the same line of work, they are a Goddamned misery as they go from corpses to us and our food. We hate the miserable bastards with a passion but cannot seem to escape them. The thin veneer that they talk about that keeps civilization from falling apart is almost non-existent, and if there really is any glory, it is not to be found here. In all our months of fighting, we have seen not one smiling face, heard not one cheer, or had even one pretty girl offer a welcome kiss.

The indifference and lack of compassion just referred to (couldn't care less about the miserable bastards is more like it) shows up as a group of us attempts to subdue a small cave. After making the initial assault, we can hear low moans coming from the interior, but there is not even the slightest thought of our going in to help this fellow human being. Instead, we continue to pour fire and toss grenades until the moaning finally ceases. I guess the worst of it is that we do this with absolutely no qualms and instead feel only relief when the son of a bitch is dead. On the other side of the ledger, if we deserve any such consideration, it is entirely possible that the SOB was merely faking in order to kill a few more of us. Such is our world.

On one of the first nights, the Japs attack in a wild banzai charge, completely overrunning some of our positions. I am dug in a canyon over from the main thrust, hear the shooting, the shouting, the explosions, and wonder what in the hell is going on. It is a mad melee in the pitch dark and many Japanese break through, but our line holds. Those who manage to get into our rear areas are eventually killed, but they take many of us with them. It is a miserable night, proving once again what a large part confusion and chaos play in this business. Daylight brings a semblance of order, but the company in that next canyon has been hit hard. Again, luck seems to have been with me, but for how long?

Confusion and chaos are, however, only part of the anguish as frustrations abound and take many forms, with one such being our enemy's particularly nasty habit of booby trapping his dead and, on occasion, even his wounded. As might be expected, this results in casualties for us as we try to tidy up after a day's advance which, of course, is the general idea. Normally, there are others who take care of these chores but, on occasion, it is up to us—the tropical climate wasting little time as it begins to put its affairs in order. So, to counter this rather low-down trick, we have come up with the idea of attaching ropes, or whatever we can find, to the aforementioned bodies and then trying to locate a safe-looking place to pull from. The idea being to move the bodies enough to set off any explosives that might be attached or under. The rotten sons of bitches then get even ornerier and begin booby trapping the most likely spots, thus adding even more misery to an already miserable job.

It has been said that World War II was a good war, and perhaps that was so, but it was not a nice war, and as a matter of fact, the "No Quarter" flag was run up early on here in the Pacific.

Late one afternoon, I get sent on another crazy jeep ride. This time, the driver and I are taking an empty water trailer back to be filled. The only passable road runs through an area still held by the Japanese, so we hold off leaving until almost dark. To make it more interesting, this so-called road is really just a wide path and full of shell holes, to boot. Finally set, my rifle at the ready, we take off with the damned trailer bouncing all over the place. How in the hell the jeep stays on the road and upright, I'll never know, but we apparently surprise the Japs and get through with little interference. Daybreak finds us heading back with our load of water, a bit more concerned about enemy fire in daylight but at least able to see the road. Barreling along in front of the lines, we attract a few shots but otherwise make it in good shape, and the company starts out with full canteens. Mighty easy work compared with attacking caves and pillboxes but still a little scary.

A few days after this little joyride, I return to my old squad. It has been hard in the lines, and many of my friends are gone; however, I am now back "home." The

Goddamned war must be getting to me, for in some strange way, I feel this is where I belong, here with my buddies. It is a world that I have become accustomed to, even though I hate it. Still, there is a certain satisfaction in just surviving this hellish life.

We get an assist from tanks when conditions permit and the things are available. Our present location, being relatively flat and containing numerous enemy positions, is one that lends Itself to that kind of support. Large areas of heavy brush, however, add an element of difficulty not apparent until the advance is well underway. With infantry trailing the tanks, the enemy, disguised by all the greenery, found that a daring soldier could slip up and slap a magnetic mine against the side of a tank before the riflemen could react—resulting in damage and much discomfort to the crew.

It was decided (not by the infantry) to have riflemen precede and flank the tanks in the hope that they could keep the enemy at bay (so to speak). In truth, the tankers were better protected with this move, however, it was now the infantry who were crying foul. The noise of the advancing Iron Beasts was unmistakable, alerting the enemy and allowing him to inflict numerous casualties on the exposed footsloggers.

With due thought then, the plan was modified once again, and the infantry went back to doing it the hard way—calling on the tanks when a particularly difficult obstacle was encountered. There really is no easy way.

Air support arrives now and then, sometimes unexpectedly. On one particular afternoon, my company is advancing through a heavily overgrown coconut grove when we hear a sudden roar of engines accompanied by cannon and machine-gun fire. Diving for cover, our first thought is that a Jap tank has somehow managed to get in behind us. In a few seconds, however, the cause of all this commotion comes into view. It turns out to be an Air Force B-25 equipped with nose cannon, and he is screaming by at treetop level, blasting away at a road junction just ahead. Apparently, someone called for air support and he, being close by, came over to assist. It was a nice thought, but we had just taken that junction, and consequently our lead squad had the hell scared out of them—it was a junction just *ahead* of this one that we had hoped to have some help with. As noted earlier, these little miscalculations are bound to happen now and then, but at least in this instance, no one was hurt. We even thought he might have scared the Japs a little. Unfortunately, we are not always this lucky, and misplaced bombs or short artillery rounds take out a few of us. It is always harder when we get hit with our own stuff, but that is the risk if we are to have close-in support.

I recall a day on Bougainville when a dive bomber put one right in our lines, killing several men. He was aiming at a spot which had been marked by smoke when the Japs threw a similar shell into our lines to confuse him and, in this case, it worked. In the long run, however, air and artillery support saves a hell of a lot more of us than it kills and, I guess, that is the bottom line.

Getting back to today's little incident, we speculate that the pilot is headed back to his base, no doubt to a hot shower and a drink before dinner. We, not being bothered by such social graces, dig our usual hole in the ground, heat up a can of hash, and prepare for another miserable night. We are moving faster now. They say the Jap is on the run—or is he hiding for another day? It is not easy, though, not yet. A buddy, thinking the danger is past, is wounded while on a search for souvenirs. It does not seem possible that the thing is almost over and that, once again, I am still in one piece.

August 10, 1944

Guam is declared secure, it is my birthday, and once again, we are allowed temporary relief from gut-wrenching fear, from constant exhaustion, and from never knowing what the next second will bring. Hunger, thirst, and misery will be forced to take a short vacation while maggots and blowflies wait impatiently for another campaign.

The end of the battle means one more time to reflect, one more time to count our crosses and to grieve for buddies whose luck ran out. And there is not even a glimmer of an end in sight. Although the fighting is officially over, it is not so for us. In our rush to take this place, thousands of the enemy were bypassed, and it will be many months before we have done with them. For some reason, the Jap does not know, or perhaps just doesn't care, that we have won the battle. Whichever it may be, he does not give up, leaving us no choice but to find and then do away with him. Unfortunately, this boils down to just more hard and dangerous work as we must root him out of hiding places in the hills and in jungle-filled canyons. The result is that there will be little rest for our already-jangled nerves.

In our spare time, we are back to building a new camp—clearing the jungle by hand, as before, and I hope to hell it is the last one. The site selected for this camp is on a beach facing eastward, and we often gaze out to sea, thinking of home a mere six thousand miles away. It might as well be a million.

Our new mosquito friends, the ones here on Guam, carry a disease called dengue fever, and I manage to come down with the damn thing. Every joint and muscle in my body aches and I am miserably sick with high fever. Malaria in the Solomons, dengue fever here, in addition to ten assorted other ailments on both islands—we fight in the damnedest places. For whatever reason, I do not turn in to the hospital and instead just sort of struggle through as best I can. It is a part of this business that we get rather accustomed to going on while sick, having learned some time ago to just endure our miseries. The sad fact is that if we were to go to sick bay or turn in to the hospital whenever we felt lousy, there would be few of us left to do the fighting. Finally, while toting a BAR on patrol (the BAR man was sicker than I), my fever breaks, and I go back to feeling more or less normal.

Patrolling continues through October, and we get to know these hills and canyons too damn well. Although most of these outings are relatively uneventful, they are damned hard work with ample doses of fear thrown in for good measure. In truth, just walking in this dense brush with the constant threat of ambush is unnerving, to say the least. And it is especially so for the point man, this being but another of the little terrors that must be experienced to be appreciated. It helps that we take turns at this miserable job, but the damn turns come around awfully fast. Funny thing though, we should, and I guess we halfway do, expect to get hit on these damned patrols, yet when it happens, it is always unexpected. For the most part, the confrontations are short and deadly, and if we are lucky, the thing is done without any of us being seriously hurt.

Once in a while, however, we take a local Chamorro along as a guide, having at least two men in front of him at all times and making sure he is not exposed any more than necessary, yet it is not always enough. On one such occasion, our patrol walks into an ambush, and the guide, though well back from the point, is nevertheless cut down. As the Japanese open up, we hit the deck, but the guide is just a little slower to react and the penalty is death. It is but another of the many small tragedies in this war; still, we view it as a rather cruel example of our hard training paying off.

Speaking of patrolling and related miseries, my group (I have just been given the rather high-sounding title of "acting corporal") is fortunate in having a guy who is sort of a natural scout. So much so, in fact, that our little group seems to be getting more than its share of the damned point business. As I have touched on before, that does get a bit old, but being one who more or less obeys orders as given, I don't make a fuss about it. To my credit, hopefully, I do spell the guy occasionally, but he seems so easy in the job that we usually wind up on the point with my buddy, in hindsight now, getting the shaft. The main problem being that we are always shorthanded so it's either that or trading with the BAR man, which is no piece of cake either.

He, however, being the class Marine that he is, never makes a big deal of it, but he does, from time to time, slip me subtle hints about sharing the Goddamned wealth. This eventually forces me to get my ass in gear and I finally bring the thing up to the squad leader. He just says, "oh hell, I didn't think you guys minded." Well, I don't know if l am ever to see my old buddy again, but if I do, he will get a belated apology.

In this miserable after-the-battle kind of warfare, we are sometimes ordered to set up ambushes at night, hoping to catch the enemy foraging for food and water. On occasion, however, it is the ambushers who sort of get ambushed. On one particular night, our three-man group is assigned an area to work in and we locate what seems to be a suitable spot just about dusk. Suddenly, shots are fired, bullets clip the leaves around us, and as daylight fades, we dive for cover in some nearby bushes. A couple more shots, then silence—a very uneasy silence.

Certain that our situation is deadly serious, we avoid any movement and strain our ears for the slightest sound. A few minutes go by, and we become aware of another problem: insects of some kind, and the damned things are all over us. Our cover, it seems, is in the middle of a Goddamned ant hill. What lousy, stinking luck! Faced now with a choice of Japs or ants, we reluctantly choose the ants. It is a long night as the pesky things crawl in our ears, noses, under our clothes, and we just have to sit there and take it. Making it worse, if the Japs knew of our misery, they would no doubt be laughing their heads off. Finally, daylight arrives and we leave the damned ants, cautiously scouting around for those responsible for our torment. There are no shots as we move about and decide the Japs must have returned to their hiding place. Wondering if we might have gone through that misery for nothing, we again come to the conclusion that war is indeed hell.

Replacement time again as new men arrive to take the place of those lost in the battle for Guam. Most are brand new, although a few had either been wounded or came down with malaria in the Guadalcanal campaign and are now back for a second grand tour. And you may be quite sure that the arrival of these "second timers" and the implication thereof is not lost on us. In addition, seeing these new men brings home, once again, a rather grim reality, and I look around my platoon, noting that of the forty men who sailed from San Diego almost two years ago, only two of us are left, and the son of a bitch is still not over. With the odds, the miserable stinking odds being what they are, it does not seem possible that I can last it out. However, and rather fortunately, I might add, we do not dwell on these things, and quite the contrary, enjoy the arrival of new men with their welcome news of home. Except for mail, which does not always find us, we know very little of what happens elsewhere, having had no liberty since New Zealand a year and a half ago. The new men settle in and we get acquainted while they bring us up to date on current events and teach us some of the latest songs. "A Lovely Way to Spend an Evening" is a favorite and seems particularly appropriate to our circumstances.

Entertainment is still pretty much a do-it-yourself kind of thing, consisting mainly of playing cards, singing, shooting the breeze, and now that things have settled down a bit, an occasional movie. Even so, with the damned Japs roaming the countryside at night, going to the movie is still somewhat of an adventure as we must carry weapons whenever leaving the immediate camp area, whether it be a trip to the movies or just a need to hit the head (go to the latrine). Though there are few encounters during these various excursions, the possibility of a knife in the back is still worrisome, and as a result, the compulsion to look over our shoulders remains a way of life.

Recreation, at least in any kind of an organized way, is still given a rather low priority, although Sunday is almost always a day off from patrolling or training, and the time after dinner is usually our own. Evenings are a time to relax, write letters, read and reread mail from home, and catch up on the many little chores that are part of our life in the field. Rifles have to be cleaned daily, tents kept neat and orderly, cots made up, and the camp area itself maintained. Evenings also are, by nature I guess, the lonesome time—the time when thoughts of home and family hit the hardest and the time when gloom and despair are the strongest.

I manage to get sick again, sick as hell this time. Too miserable to fight it any longer, I turn in to the hospital, which is just a large tent in a jungle clearing. You must have at least a 102-degree fever to be admitted, and I am just over the requirement. Damn near too sick to stand but it doesn't matter, I still have to go into the nearby jungle and cut four sticks to hold up my mosquito netting before being directed to one of the canvas cots. Nice round sticks are made for this purpose, but what else is new?

Over the next few days, I run a very high temperature, either shaking with chills or sweating with fever, and sleep most of the time. I finally come out of it to find that I have been moved to the critical ward, which is merely the front of the tent. My dungarees and mattress pad are soaked with sweat, and I stink to high heaven. A dose of malaria followed by yellow jaundice, and it's doubtful that I could have just struggled through this one.

While recuperating, an old buddy is brought in and assigned a cot next to mine. We shared a foxhole for a few days during the latter stages of the Bougainville campaign. It was a time of heavy enemy shelling along with many casualties, and we went through some terrifying yet occasionally funny moments. On one of these, Japanese artillery opened up just as we began heating a canteen cup of chocolate on a small heat-tab stove in the front of our foxhole. We lay on our backs, as the shelling started, trying to figure a way to stir the chocolate without getting killed. We could hear the guns fire, then the shells would explode about a second later, sometimes too damn close for comfort. We finally decided to take turns sitting up, stirring the chocolate and then, after hearing the guns fire, trying to get back down before the shells exploded. We didn't always succeed, but luck must have been with us. As I recall, the chocolate tasted mighty good. We joked about this many times, always a little amazed that we could risk it all for such a small pleasure.

Now, all of a sudden, there is talk of a plan to rotate a few old-timers back to the States, with names to be drawn from a list of men having a specified amount of combat and overseas time. Those of us who came over with the division are eligible, and for the first time, going home is a distinct possibility instead of a dream. From where we sit, the war seems as though it could go on forever and, up until now, the only way back was as a casualty. However, the rules have suddenly been changed and we can think of nothing else. In addition, rumor has it that two of the men chosen from my company are here in the hospital. There being only three of us, I can almost see myself walking down that gangplank in San Francisco.

Finally, the magic day arrives, and the first name read off is that of my buddy in the next cot. What luck, he is in seventh heaven. I am so sure of being next that I just wait for the words. The man finally calls out the last name, but it is not mine. Instead, the name belongs to a guy who is grinning from ear to ear and who just happens to be a couple of cots away on the other side of me. I'm stunned; luck has hit all around but missed me completely. In a very real sense, this little drawing has been a deadly kind of lottery with the winners having a chance at life while the losers, well, the losers are back in Hell—at least that's the way it looked at the time.

However, I begin to feel that it was probably too good to be true and assume there must still be a bit of misery left in my cup. After a few more days in the hospital, I return to my company and my lucky friends go home.

As Guadalcanal did before it, Guam takes on a semblance of civilization as it rapidly becomes our main forward base in the Central Pacific. What changes have taken place this past year—but what a terrible cost, and the worst may still be ahead. However, for now at least, the PX is open, things are looking up a little, and I am able to enjoy an occasional cigar again—a two- or three-hour wait in line notwithstanding. The place has the usual candy bars, personal gear, and so on, but strange as it may seem, a couple of the most popular items are soda crackers and small cans of pork and beans. Must be something lacking in our diet—like food, maybe. Then, every couple of weeks or so, we get a ration of beer or Coca-Cola and that is the real treat, even though it is as warm as the weather.

And now, as an indication of just how routine things are getting, the regimental commander decides to hold a rifle match, and I am one of two selected to represent our company. It is somewhat of an honor, but unfortunately, I am washed out before even firing a shot. Turns out there are too many shooters for the time allotted, so those with boot camp scores under a certain figure are rather unceremoniously eliminated. Another small disappointment is thus added to my store of such things, and I report back feeling that I have somehow let the company down. Life, at least by our standards, has become rather tolerable, although we wonder for how long.

Now, rumors of a new operation begin drifting around camp, and they are saying it will be a tough one, worse than anything so far. God, how I envy those lucky devils who are going home, and I wonder again how long my luck can last. Training is intensified as we attack simulated pillboxes and strongpoints, using the latest flamethrowers in addition to BARs, machine guns, and demolition charges. We also spend considerable time with flame-throwing tanks and, though they appear to be a very handy tool, they most likely will not be around when needed. In addition, individual firepower has been noticeably increased, with each squad now having three (Browning) automatic rifles plus a flamethrower and demolition charges. Even though this stuff will surely be helpful, it is heavy as hell, and the result is that the poor old foot slogger's job just gets tougher and tougher. The damn flamethrowers, in particular, are a mixed blessing, and they will no doubt save some of us; however, the poor devil who carries one is likely to have a short life. With good reason, the Japanese make his elimination a high priority. It is hell that we must use these terrible weapons, but the enemy, in his selection of a hold-out-to-the-bitter-end defense, gives us little choice. It comes down to them or us, and most of the time it's both of us.

Returning late, bushed and beat as usual from one of those long training sessions, a strange thing happens as our raggedy-assed column moves out of some low trees. Rounding a sharp bend just ahead comes a jeep with, of all things, two gals and a couple of Navy officers (lucky bastards). The young ladies look to be from a USO tour or perhaps—hell, who cares where they're from, they are lovely. We quickly recall that it has been all of a year and a half, way back in New Zealand, since we have seen anything like that up close, and it really is a case of culture shock. We, in our sweat-soaked dungarees, loaded down with the mean and deadly tools of our trade, having almost forgotten them (just kidding). They, looking so pretty, so immaculate, so utterly feminine. That sudden look of surprise, however, betraying the fact that they never expected to actually come face to face with the grubby world that rumor held to be out here somewhere. Although just a split-second meeting of the eyes, in that instant, we catch a glimpse of that other world. And, for a rather large number of us, that brief look, that tiny accidental encounter will have to do, for there will not be another in this lifetime.

I am promoted to corporal, made assistant squad leader, and assigned to the flamethrower and demolition group. The war seems to be getting meaner as we move closer to Japan, and if the rumors are correct, the foot sloggers are going to take a hellish beating in this next one. Thanksgiving and Christmas pass with little in the way of celebration, though as always, we make the best of it and enjoy what we have. Who knows if we are to see another, and the reality is that many of us will not. The really important things are the mail and our ever-welcomed packages from home. The packages are often smashed or broken, but the contents are savored to the last crumb and are always shared with the rest of the tent. Mail is a little different, and while some seem to enjoy sharing their letters, most look on this as a private time, with each word being read and reread countless times. Mail call is, of course, a happy time, but underneath there is always a note of sadness, for it is our only contact with that other world—a world that seems ever more unattainable.

IWO JIMA

Over time, the sweetness of victory will
come second to relief from misery and fear.

February 1945

Rumors of an upcoming battle having once more been confirmed, we are on the move again as I begin my third year in the boondocks. As before, our seabags have been packed for storage, although on this occasion, we are thankfully unaware of just how few will return to unpack them. There is a saying about ignorance being bliss, and it is certainly true in our case. Finally, then, with combat packs in order, weapons and gear once again ready, we say goodbye to another comfortable camp, then proceed to the embarkation area and board the USS *Fayette*. There is the usual wisecracking and rough humor as we move out; however, I also note a somberness that hadn't been apparent on other such days and wonder if this could be due to a growing realization that this really is going to be a tough son of a bitch.

Then, after taking on their complement of men and equipment, the transports weigh anchor, form up in convoy with our escort vessels, and put to sea. Heading north once again, sleek destroyers, cruisers, submarines, and support craft of all types maneuver into assigned positions as stately carriers keep watch from the horizon, and in the middle of it all, our rather untidy group of transports. Although we have been a part of these giant armadas before, it is always an inspiring sight and one that never fails to raise the hair on our necks. War is so terrible and yet so magnificent.

Duty notwithstanding, these flashy men of war most likely resent this rather unglamorous assignment, having seemingly been demoted, ordered to play nursemaid to a bunch of lowly transports, and it no doubt hurts their pride. The word is out, however, that we are valuable cargo, and in addition, rumor has it that a particularly large amount of misery will go to waste should we fail to reach our destination.

This time, unlike the feeling aboard ship as we sailed for Bougainville, there is no deceptive calm, no wondering what combat is all about. The old-timers in particular, having tasted the bitterness, know only too well they just don't know how bad it will be. Then, with the maneuvering for position finally completed, the ships move out, and as the convey clears Guam, we are told that our objective is a place called Iwo Jima, a rather small island in the volcano chain. The Fourth and Fifth Marine Divisions are to make the initial landing on February 19. Our division, the Third, is to stand offshore as floating reserve and go in as needed. With three Marine Divisions in one battle, we are certain it's going to be tough, especially after learning that the damn place is only a little over four miles long by two and a half miles wide, and that is at its widest.

Luck of the draw, or whatever you will, is going to put some eighty thousand American and Japanese men on this crummy piece of rock in a fight to the finish, and of that number, fifty thousand will be killed or wounded. The Japanese will die almost to a man while the Marine rifle companies are going to have the living hell kicked out of them.

Then, to give us a sense of the place and a brief look at the lay of the land, squad and group leaders are each issued a small battle map showing two completed airfields, Motoyama Number One and Number Two, plus another under construction. There is a volcano at the southern tip named Mount Suribachi and the rest of the island slopes toward high ground in the north. The enemy will look down on us all the way, and there will be no place to hide.

We adjust to shipboard life as usual, accepting saltwater showers, long lines, and crowded quarters along with the other "comforts" these homes away from home provide. This being the ninth such trip for me, I'm beginning to feel as if half my life has been spent on these buckets. Though each ship is somewhat different, the routine stays pretty much the same, with the Corps wanting to keep us busy and pissed off whenever possible, and one of the many ways they accomplish both is by having us stand watches in various parts of the ship. We guard the heads, the drinking fountains, the ladders, all kinds of screwy places.

On this trip, I draw the midnight-to-four watch on the boat deck, and although I am not altogether sure what I am supposed to be guarding up there, it doesn't really matter; the important thing is that I am guarding something. After a short nap, I put on my helmet and cartridge belt (that's orders) then head for the galley and a hot cup of joe (coffee). Our pleasures are not many, but that cup of joe as we go on watch does hit the spot.

As you might expect, my rather isolated post is a lonely one on this watch, and along with this loneliness and the fact that Iwo is only six hundred miles from Japan comes an unaccustomed chill as we move into these dangerous northern waters. Our years in the tropics no doubt have something to do with it, but I wonder if some of this chill might perchance be due to more than the weather. As there is little to do except walk my post, I often look past landing craft hanging in davits, out across the dark water, and gaze at the faint outlines of nearby ships. No lights showing in these troubled waters, while the only sounds are of the ship straining and creaking as she makes her way through the seas and, of course, the ever-present ship's bell ringing out the half hour of each watch.

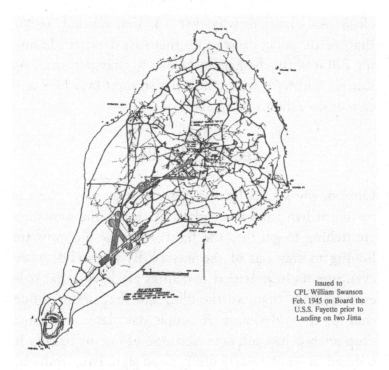

Issued to
CPL William Swanson
Feb. 1945 on Board the
U.S.S. Fayette prior to
Landing on Iwo Jima

I received this map as did all squad and assistant squad leaders prior to the Iwo Jima invasion. It was the only time we were provided a map.>

The ocean, always ominous at night, somehow seems even more so this trip, and I imagine this has to do with the danger we face and our rather uncertain fate. On those dark, moonless nights especially, I feel an almost overpowering sense of gloom and, in this mood, find it damn hard to see any light in the tunnel.

Now, with our voyage nearing its inevitable end, my thoughts turn often to home and family, yet I become less and less certain of ever seeing them again. Home. Even the thought gets dimmer in the time and distance. The convoy, however, cares little for such trivia, being concerned only with a particular heading as it takes us closer and closer to whatever it is that waits. It seems that we are being drawn into that vast darkness, knowing full well the danger yet unable to change course. As if in a nightmare, we are heading straight into Hell and cannot do a damn thing about it.

February 19, 1945

Our convoy stands by, some distance away, as the invasion of lwo Jima takes place. As usual, the new men are itching to get into the fight while the old guys are hoping to stay out of the misery. By day's end, however, rumors have it that casualties are heavy, that it is even tougher than we thought, and that doesn't bode well for the old-timers. A couple days later, our ships drop anchor just offshore and one of our regiments is ordered in—not a particularly good sign. Iwo, from our vantage point aboard ship, has the look of Hell. The damn place is barren and reeky with a sinister, almost evil look as it sits under a layer of smoke and dust. The look of the thing is bad enough, but it is even worse that there seems to be no letup in the fighting as battle wagons continue to pound away at targets and Corsairs fire rockets in support of the rifle companies.

The following day, February 23, we watch and cheer as "Old Glory" is raised on Mount Suribachi. Our spirits go up along with the flag hut, but by late afternoon, reality returns as we get word that our regiment has been ordered to land in the morning. The flag raising had given us a bit of hope, but this is it, and there is no more thought of our staying out of the Goddamned thing.

Once again, we take advantage of a last evening aboard ship, staying by the rail a little later than usual as we shoot the breeze, watch the flashes of artillery fire, and think about tomorrow. The old-timers look back to our first combat landing, a century or two ago, and sense that something is missing on this occasion. The anticipation of high adventure has somehow disappeared, no doubt lost with our discovery of misery and fear, and has pretty much been replaced by a feeling of "do what has to be done and get the son of a bitch over with."

Morning arrives, and we climb down the nets into our waiting landing craft as I again think of other landings and wonder how many more lay ahead. Even the new men appear somewhat subdued as we make our way to the beach, though they have yet to appreciate the finer points of the terror to come. The old-timers, on the other hand, know the Goddamned odds are catching up with us and fear that our luck must run out sometime but are still determined to see the thing through—all the while hoping like hell that those miserable odds can be overcome.

The coxswain drops the ramp, and we walk into a scene of utter destruction—even more so than on Guam. The beach is littered with remains of landing craft, tanks, am-tracs, equipment of all kinds, and the damned island looks even worse up close than it did from the ship. Working parties unload supplies as best they can in the face of more-or-less constant shelling; however, it is just a prelude for us as the Japs are concentrating most of their fire on the attacking infantry. Sporadic or not, the Goddamned explosions and resultant flying debris soon bring on that old gut-grabbing fear. God, what a miserable feeling! In addition, we are loaded down with weapons, ammo, and heavy gear, making this little stroll through shifting volcanic ash a difficult one. Nevertheless, we eventually make it to a spot near Airfield Number One, a few hundred yards from the front lines, and are ordered to dig in for the night. The regiment that landed a couple of days ago has taken part of Airfield Number Two and suffered terrible casualties in the process. We are to relieve them in the morning and continue the advance.

Then, as we prepare to dig in, one of those God-damned rocket-launching trucks suddenly skids to a stop nearby. We know what's coming and wish to hell he would leave and do his business someplace else, but it is too late as he quickly fires his deadly load and takes off in a cloud of dust. "Dirty rotten son of a bitch, we're gonna get it now!" Sure enough, in less than a minute, Jap artillery returns the favor. Another little preview of things to come as we get the hell scared out of us and our first casualties.

Digging in this loose volcanic ash proves difficult and frustrating, so most of us just take what cover we can find in the many bomb craters. The miserable shelling continues all night, allowing little sleep and doing nothing for our morale. If we ever had any illusions about this battle, they are fast fading away with our chances looking more and more like a tossup between slim and none. And bad as it may seem, these odds are really not too far off the mark. Our squad landed with ten men and, of those ten, seven will be killed and the other three wounded.

Vehicle-mounted rockets vehicles on Iwo Jima.

Unfortunately, these numbers will not be uncommon in the rifle platoons, however, even if we knew, which thank God we don't, I doubt anything would change. More than anything else, we are committed to each other—and, of course, the damned Corps. Something happens along the way, and I don't quite know what it is, but the man next to you is certain that you will be there, and you know damn well he will be there.

In addition, we pray that God allows us to survive, and we pray that He gives us the courage to keep going. Jackets have been issued to wear over our dungarees, but they are not enough as we shiver from the cold, or is it fear, or maybe both. I can't remember shivering from fear, but it may be that I have been out here too long.

Eventually, daylight arrives, and we greet the day with mixed feelings—glad the miserable night is over, yet fearful of what the morning will bring. Breakfast is as usual, being hash or stew along with some hard crackers and will no doubt be the last meal for many, but again—which ones? Not yet burdened by the gut-wrenching fear to come, we chat about small things while we feast on our sumptuous meal and gripe about the many and varied items that we are blessed with to gripe about. We even find room for a small chuckle when someone mentions that he heard it's getting really tough back in the States, with long lines and shortages. The talk, he says, is that all the good stuff is going to the troops overseas. We look around, trying to remember what the good stuff looked like and allow ourselves another chuckle. We make a pact over cold coffee that when the war is over we will all meet in San Francisco for a get-together.

"Second platoon, knock off the Goddamned crap and get your gear on—we're movin' out." We have moved out to other battles on other mornings, but this place is different. If there is a piece of Hell anywhere on Earth, this must be it. What little brush left standing has been torn and mangled, shell holes and bomb craters are everywhere, and the worst of it is that new ones crop up almost every second. Looking toward the front lines, there is no sign of life, but it is certain that our enemy is waiting, that he is expecting us, and that he is ready.

My regiment moving up to airfield #2 in preparation to attack.

We move out in single file, hugging the abutment along the edge of Airfield Number One, then, as we pass between the two airfields and become more visible to the enemy, he welcomes us with increased artillery. The morning is off to one hell of a start as we proceed up to and then alongside Airfield Number Two, trying as best we can to put the explosions out of our minds, and then, with a rather abrupt suddenness, we are the front lines. Our other regiment having been pulled back into reserve, it is now up to us. We are positioned at the bottom of a rather steep abutment forming one side of the airfield and will start our advance from here. My regiment, with two battalions abreast, will make the main effort against the enemy's center.

Taking advantage of what cover is available, we wait and worry as enemy fire increases. Then, as time (for us) winds down, squad leaders and assistants are called together for last-minute instructions—a finality of sorts. In a place like this, each movement carries risk, so we hurry to our meeting in one of the many shell holes, crouching down low as we get the word. Our orders are simple and quite clear: attack across the runway above with a particular emphasis on the fact that this objective must be taken. It is also stressed that enemy fire will be extremely heavy on the airfield, making it imperative that we fight our way across in as short a time as possible. Dodge, weave, hit the deck, then get up and do it again. Easy to say but may not be that easy to do. It is a short meeting, too short in a way, and as the impact of what we are to do begins to sink in, my squad leader and I look at each other for one brief second, then dash back to the squad and get set to advance on orders. There is no time now for thoughts of home and little opportunity to think of our future or if we are to have one as fear of the exploding shells overrides almost everything else.

"Fix bayonets" comes down the line, followed by the sound of a thousand blades being pulled from scabbards and then a series of clicks as they are fitted to rifles. Weapons are now given one final check, making doubly sure that a round is in the chamber and that the safely is off—this being no time for stupid mistakes. Once again waiting out that little lull, we hug the ground, fearful but ready, without the slightest doubt as to who will carry the day.

Suddenly, a raised arm gives the signal, platoon and squad leaders yell, "Let's go," and the line moves out. Hundreds of men, rifles at the ready, climb the ten or so feet to the airstrip and start running. Some are yelling, most are simply engrossed in trying to survive, we rush into the unknown, rush into Hell, and in a few seconds, all hell really does break loose. Some are cut down almost immediately as high-velocity anti-tank and anti-aircraft guns begin firing from high ground to our right; machine guns open up in front while artillery and mortar shells explode in our midst.

Terror is constant and everywhere as the rest of us run, hit the deck, then get up and run again. The air is filled with dust, dirt, and chunks of hot metal; the damned runway is a mass of craters and debris. To say that this is not a nice place is to mock the very meaning of understatement. Even so, there is a feeling that we must go on as long as possible, although it becomes increasingly difficult to focus on anything but our own little world. We are in a crowd of sorts yet feel so alone—only God and us.

Advancing into this more-or-less constant mayhem, our raggedy green line gets thinner but seldom stops. However, all sense of time has disappeared, having been lost somewhere in this struggle to stay alive and to kill. Afraid every second, the noise, the earth-shaking explosions, are almost more than we can bear.

The attack is a blur of slit trenches, emplacements, shell holes—the Goddamn Jap won't give it up. When will I get hit? How bad will it be? Which step will be my last? I try to be the good Marine but—please, God—if it is to be, make it quick. Finally across the miserable runway, we again hug the ground for dear life and wait for orders to move on. Just ahead is another abutment and God only knows what beyond that. Lying flat on my stomach, I try to be as small a target as possible, but the explosions are devastating. Now, orders come down for us to take whatever cover we can while the battalion regroups for the next push. It is frustrating as hell, this never knowing where the sons of bitches are going to hit. Should I move and try to better my position, or might it be worse somewhere else? A few men jump into a large bomb crater on my left, maybe I should join them. Then, before I can make up my mind, a shell lands in the Goddamn crater, killing them all. It is absolute hell. I cannot think—I can only pray.

This waiting under fire, while the various units get organized, is hard as hell, and our casualties mount. A couple of men are ordered to climb the abutment and try to find out where all this Goddamned crap is coming from. They are killed as they raise their heads to look. A short time later, a machine-gun crew throws their weapon on top of the same abutment to give some covering fire and, one by one, are struck as they try to get in position to fire. There is no place to hide and no way to escape the Goddamned misery. I watch as a buddy is killed a few yards to my right, hugging the ground like I am but in an unlucky spot. I pray, please God please God, wondering all the while how much longer for me?

Suddenly, my right hand feels like it has been hit with a hammer. Uh-oh. I look quickly to see how bad it is. There is a rather jagged cut on the back of my right hand and through the webbing of my thumb and index finger partially severing both digits but little blood, and if there is any pain, I don't notice. I let the squad leader know that I have been hit and that it doesn't look too bad. He tells me to move up to the abutment and have a corpsman check it out. Carrying my rifle in my left hand, I make the short dash as ordered. The corpsmen are all busy, so I wait. Finally, one gets free and dashes over for a look. Time being a problem and my wound being a minor one, he applies sulfa powder, wraps my hand, and tags me to see a doctor at the battalion aid station. For some screwy reason, however, I decide to stay with my squad for the time being, not really sure that I have been hit bad enough to be sent back. It is rather odd, though, now that I have been given an excuse to get away from this hellish place, I discover that leaving my buddies is not the easy thing I thought it would be.

At the time, this strange reluctance to seek at least relative safety when offered seemed to be merely a small case of craziness in a crazy place, but I have since been told of men who, after being wounded, literally had to be dragged from the lines. Again, then, I find that in all this hell, the line between fear and duty is a fine and sometimes blurry one and assume that our feelings for each other and the "damned Corps" are probably beyond understanding. A short time later, our platoon leader races over and dives down beside us. He tells the squad leader and me to get the men ready, that we're moving out in a few minutes. Then he looks at my bandaged hand, points at me jabbing his finger while saying, "You get the hell out of here, I don't want any Goddamn cripples where we're going."

That was that. I say goodbye to those close by and wish them luck. Our parting words are, "I'll see you in Frisco." The hell of it is that the battle for Iwo does not get any better, and only a few make it to the Golden Gate.

On my own now, I steel myself for the return trip and get set to cross the damned runway again. Then, as I turn around for one last look, I am struck by the fact that, for the first time in two and a half years, I will not be going where the second platoon goes. It is no doubt a blessing, though I will surely leave a part of me on this miserable, Godforsaken rock. However, my small reverie is soon ended by fear, and with this return to reality, I notice a couple of seriously wounded being strapped to stretchers for the trip back and decide to go along for company. There is little or no letup in the damned artillery and mortar fire as we start out, and it is just one more of those hard truths that many wounded will be hit again before reaching safety.

I don't know how many times we hit the deck or how long we spend on this little trek, but I can't help feeling sorry for those poor devils on the stretchers. Though the bearers try to be careful and considerate, it is beyond them. With the best of intentions, they stumble and fall as they dodge shell holes and explosions, on occasion are hit themselves, and at the same time, they worry constantly about their precious cargo. It is the nature of this business that, at one time or another, most of us are called on to perform this task, and it is hard work at best. Under heavy fire, such as today, it is miserably hard work.

Getting back to my personal predicament, my sore hand gets banged around as we dive down and fall down but is hardly worth noting on this kind of day. Then, after hitting the deck one particular time, I look up to find that in this desperate need to seek cover, I have lost contact with my companions and am now completely alone on this desolate piece of Hell. We hadn't said a word, but it was comforting just being with someone. They say that to be alone in a crowd is a terrible feeling; I am not sure what they would say about being alone in Hell. Either way, there is little doubt that misery does indeed love company.

I am not sure how or why, but I eventually reach the edge of the runway, dive off the embankment at a run, and land in a heap at the bottom. Here I am, back where it all started this morning, but everything looks so different now. There is no sign of an aid station, or anyone else for that matter, and except for the exploding shells, I may as well be on another planet.

However, it isn't long before I manage to get somewhat oriented and brace myself for the next part of my journey. The shelling is less intense than on the airfield but is still too heavy for comfort as I take off running again, diving in and out of shell holes, and finding it harder and harder to leave them. I can find a dozen reasons for staying in these safe little havens and being all alone; who would know? Pride, however, or training, or perhaps a little of both keeps kicking me in the butt, forcing me to move on. It is a hard way to earn a living, though, and not without some close calls. Once, as a shell explodes nearby, I dive for a crater just as another lands even closer. It is eerie as hell, for in that brief instant, I am looking right at the damn thing as it goes off, see the *V* shape of the explosive force, and feel the rush of air but no hot metal. Thanks, God.

"You okay, Mac?" a voice from the crater asks. Crawling safely into the crater, I find company—a Gyrene from a reserve unit just moving up. He had been watching my progress, saw the shells explode, and couldn't believe I was still in one piece. How much luck can I have left? We chat for a few minutes, then he has to leave, and as we wish each other luck, he moves out and I try to screw up my courage for another dash. This last little incident shook me just a bit, and I lie down, hugging my old friend the ground, wishing that I didn't have to leave. But I soon feel that old kick in the ass and reluctantly get on my way. After a few more of these mad dashes, I finally locate an aid station and am retagged for evacuation. Then, leaving the worst of the shelling behind, I head for the beach and by late afternoon join the, by now, quite large number of casualties waiting their turn to be transported out to ships for further treatment.

In due time, although it always seems longer, the inevitable processing is completed, and a group of us are directed to an amphibious truck called a duck (DUKW). Those with serious wounds are lifted aboard on stretchers while the rest of us help each other and get on as best we can. Then, as the truck bounces down the beach and drives into the surf, those who are able look back at and marvel that we are still alive. Deep down, there is sadness at leaving our buddies after all we have been through and knowing, all too well, how hard the going will be. On the other hand, we feel lucky to have survived and silently give thanks to God. Leaving Iwo behind does not end all our problems, however, as we are forced to spend some time trying to find a ship that has room for more wounded. And, with some of our group in critical condition, it is disappointing to find that the hospital ships are already full, and so far at least, the same has been true for the troop transports. Though we are certain that everyone is doing the best they can under these less-than-ideal conditions, we are beginning to be really concerned about our seriously injured when the USS *Doyen* finally signals that she can take us aboard. One by one, we are placed on stretchers and hoisted on deck by winch, the serious cases first and then the walking wounded like myself.

After the doctors have finished with those most in need, I get my turn and am taken to the ship's small hospital for treatment. The operating room, located deep in the bowels of the ship, is dark except for a bright light over the operating table. There is a sense and a fear of suffering as I am led into this room, and for some strange reason, I have the strong impression of being back in some medieval time, thinking how difficult and painful it must have been for the wounded.

Then, very quickly, two huge blood-covered men roughly force me onto the table, strap my right arm down, and proceed to hold me in a vise-like grip—there being no anesthetic for the more or less minor wounds. It seems very cold and businesslike, yet I sense that, underneath it all, they understand where we have been. It's just that the personal touch has been lost in the number of casualties coming off Iwo. It takes only a couple of minutes as the "Doc" probes for shrapnel or debris, but I see why they hold me down; it hurts like hell, and I find myself wondering how many he has worked on today.

A corpsman wraps my hand and directs me to the sick bay where I am assigned a bunk and told to wait for further orders. During the next few days, the doctors will be weeding out those who can be sent back into action—the meat grinder, you see, is still hungry. What makes it especially hard is the grim knowledge that many of those selected will be going back to their deaths. To get this far and then to have to return is probably worse than going in at first, for we now know the hell that is out there. Even so, there is no complaining from those going back, at least not outwardly—our real fears are kept to ourselves. One morning a group of us walking wounded are escorted by a doctor and taken up on deck for screening to return to battle. As the process goes on and those who are selected move over to one side of the deck, I realize the attention of the staff doing the selecting has now focused on me. A hand motions me to join those going back. The doctor who escorted us to the deck was behind me and speaking with someone as this occurred. As I began to move toward the group the doctor placed his hand on my shoulder and stated "Corporal Swanson has been running a high fever and isn't ready to return yet." The malarial fever spike or residual fever from dengue fever a couple of months back and the still fresh wound to my hand which would have made firing a rifle difficult kept me on board.

Then, after a few days on the *Doyen*, a number of us are transferred to the USS *President Adams* for further evacuation. She is taking a load of wounded to the hospital on Saipan, has one damaged screw and able to make only half her normal speed, but she is headed in the right direction. I remain in the hospital on Saipan for a few days then, due to the large number of casualties still arriving from Iwo, am placed with a group being transferred to the naval hospital in Pearl Harbor. The hospitals in the Western Pacific are filling up, and the upcoming invasion of Okinawa is expected to bring thousands more. Still, there is no end in sight.

We board the USS *Karnes* as I add yet another voyage to my itinerary and, for the first time, allow myself the luxury of thinking that I might actually make it. I even dare think about that magic ship, the one that takes you home. For the most part, however, the ten-day trip to Hawaii is a pleasant one with the only discouraging event coming with the crossing of the International Date Line. Anxious as we are to reach civilization, it is a bit disappointing to find that a day is gained when sailing east. We hit the sack one night only to wake up in the morning and find that it is still the same day as it was yesterday.

And, with the subject at hand being minor tragedies, I may as well mention that I have no money. I never thought about needing money when we left for Iwo, but here I am with the ship's store open, a rarity on other voyages, and no way to enjoy the treats. Haven't had ice cream in I don't know how long, and cigars—how I would love to stand by the rail and—well, as you can no doubt see, there are tortures and then there are tortures. In our organization, however, these misfortunes are explained and more or less accepted with the simple phrase: "Such is life in the Corps."

There is no band and no celebration, at least not for us, as we dock in Pearl Harbor. A shipload of wounded is not a particularly pleasant sight, I guess, so we are just quietly transported to the naval hospital at Aiea Heights. In a few days, it's mostly paperwork now, I am released and transferred to the Marine Corps Transient Center. This is a large pool of men waiting for the winds of fate to decide their future, and I imagine most will be heading west, with a good many replacing those lost on Iwo. I remain in this camp for a week or ten days, still not sure which direction I am headed, still not letting myself think home.

Finally, orders are posted for me to report to the processing office for transfer. As usual, there is a long line of men waiting to hear what kind of hand fate has dealt them. Then, as I get closer to the front of the line, I can hear some of the questions being asked of each man, and the important ones seem to be how long have you been overseas and how many campaigns do you have under your belt? Most, it appears, are relative short-timers with few having been in more than one battle and many yet to see action. These men receive orders taking them west. My turn, and I answer twenty-seven months and three campaigns. The interviewer looks at me for a few seconds and then says just four beautiful words: "Mac, you're going home."

Just like that, it was over; the misery and the hell of the last two years is finally over and "I made it." Though I am jumping for joy on the inside, I take the news calmly, almost cautiously, still afraid that at the last minute it will somehow be taken away. Just a small case of too many pulled-out rugs, I suspect.

However, it now appears that I really have attained the unattainable and, with that, my thoughts quickly turn to those who were not so fortunate, and I sense much of my elation slipping away. I feel so lucky yet constantly wonder how these things are decided. There must be a plan, though I cannot believe that I am more important or more deserving than those who are lost. Those nearby congratulate me on my good fortune. "You lucky bastard, you lucky son of a bitch, what I wouldn't give to be in your shoes." It is over, but it is not quite over—not yet. The word is that I will be in a rifle company for the invasion of Japan. But that is tomorrow, today is now, and I am going home. A few days later, still looking over my shoulder, I board that magic ship, the USS *Matsonia*, bound for San Francisco.

IN REPLYING ADDRESS
COMMANDANT OF THE MARINE CORPS
WASHINGTON 25, D. C.
AND REFER TO

SERIAL
468731
DGU-893-sem

HEADQUARTERS U. S. MARINE CORPS
WASHINGTON

24 March, 1945.

My dear Mr. Swanson:

  A report has just been received that your son, Corporal William K. Swanson, USMC, was wounded in action against the enemy at Iwo Jima, Volcano Islands. The report further states that he was removed for medical treatment.

  Because of the great volume of communications now required for essential military operations, the report received was necessarily brief and did not disclose the extent of his injuries. It is hoped that he will communicate with you soon, informing you of his welfare.

  Your anxiety is realized, and you may be sure that any additional information received will be forwarded to you at the earliest possible moment. Meanwhile, you have been furnished all the facts available, and you will help this Headquarters send out subsequent reports promptly if you will write only to notify this office of any change in your address.

     Sincerely yours,

      D. ROUTH,
    Major, U. S. Marine Corps.

Mr. William E. Swanson,
  3432 Rosemary Avenue,
    Glendale, California.

POSTSCRIPT

With the war in the Pacific still appearing to be far from over, I was being rotated to the states for a bit of R&R, then to be shipped back out to start it all over again. There was not even a thought, much less a hope, of remaining stateside as it was made abundantly clear that I would be in a rifle company for the invasion of Japan.

The atomic bomb changed everything. For the Japanese in Hiroshima and Nagasaki, it was a horror beyond imagination, as is war in general for those who are forced to grovel in it. For us, however, and for a great many Japanese, the atomic bomb simply meant life, and from a personal point of view, I doubt this story could have been written without it.

1945. Home after twenty-seven months in the Pacific and fifty pounds lighter.

*"On the beach of bloody Iwo Jima,
a wounded Marine was asked if he
managed to bring back any souvenirs.
The Marine thought for a moment—
yeah, mac, my ass. I got out with my ass."*

And that pretty much says it all.

Me in 1989, at the time I wrote this book.

ABOUT THE AUTHOR

William "Bill" Swanson was born in August 1924 in Taft, California. His parents, William E. and Helen Sall, were first generation children of Swedish immigrant farmers. Helen died tragically a couple of weeks after the birth of their second son, Glen, in 1926. Then in Glendale, California, a single father with an infant and young son, William tried desperately to provide for his boys and keep his job, hiring housekeepers and neighbors to watch the boys.

Ultimately raised by their loving grandmother, Bill and Glen remained there until the outbreak of WWII and Bill's enlistment in the United States Marine Corps.

After the war, Bill returned to Glendale where he met his future wife Rita Dolores Rockefeller. They married in Santa Barbara and took their honeymoon along the coast to San Francisco. They bought a small house in the orange grove suburbs of L.A., raised two children, and later had two grandchildren and two great-grandchildren. Bill retired from the City of Los Angeles Water & Power Dept. in 1986. In retirement, they enjoyed 3rd Marine Division reunions where they made many close friends. They had a wonderful life together. Rita passed away in 2013 and Bill now lives near his family in Imperial Beach, California